P9-ECZ-054

The Cost of Capital

The Cost of Capital
Estimating the Rate of Return for Public Utilities

A. Lawrence Kolbe and
James A. Read, Jr.
with George R. Hall

A Charles River Associates Study

The MIT Press
Cambridge, Massachusetts
London, England

Charles River Associates, a Boston-based firm founded in 1965, provides consulting to business, government, and the legal profession on economic, technological, and management issues. The firm's professional staff includes economists, financial experts, operations research specialists, transportation experts, engineers, and computer scientists. CRA's work covers a wide spectrum, including fuel industry, electric power, and energy economics; industry regulation; economic/engineering feasibility studies for new ventures; international trade; market forecasting for metals, minerals, and other commodities; market research for products and services; antitrust policy; communications; science and technology policy; transportation planning; and strategic planning for a broad range of industries.

Second printing, 1985

This book was set in Linotron Palatino by Achorn Graphic Services, Inc., and printed and bound by Halliday Lithograph in the United States of America.

Library of Congress Cataloging in Publication Data

Kolbe, A. Lawrence.
The cost of capital, estimating the rate of return for public utilities.

Bibliography: p.
Includes index.
1. Public utilities—Rate of return. 2. Public utilities—Finance. I. Read, James A. II. Hall, George R. III. Title.
HD2763.K64 1984 338.4'33636 84-12241
ISBN 0-262-11094-6

Contents

Preface

The genesis of this book was an effort by the California Public Utilities Commission (CPUC) to understand better the principal methods used to determine the appropriate rate of return for utility investors. Specifically, the CPUC commissioned Charles River Associates Incorporated (CRA) to analyze and critique the various approaches to estimating the cost of equity capital and to explore their use in establishing rates of return for utilities. One result of this effort was a report (cited in the references) that conveyed the results of the investigation to the CPUC. As a separate part of the contract, the results also were presented in training workshops for the CPUC staff.

The goal of the project was to provide the CPUC staff with technical information and analysis to assist them in preparing, evaluating, or critiquing rate of return recommendations using the various cost of capital estimation methods. The CPUC explicitly directed the project not to select a "preferred" estimation method, but rather to try to provide the best understanding possible of the various techniques and their relative advantages and disadvantages for regulatory purposes.

While the project's goals were satisfied, the report that resulted was subject to the limitations of working under a fixed time and budget constraint. The CPUC staff had the opportunity to obtain more detail and ask questions at the workshops, so the report was prepared as a handbook, using an outline format and stating many points tersely. Even so, the report seems to have received wide attention inside and outside California, and we frequently get requests for copies, as well as comments and questions on its contents.

This interest has led us to present the subject matter of the report in a more self-contained manner through this book. We have also taken the opportunity to improve the contents of the CPUC report in several areas. Much of the material in this book and the CPUC Report is the same, but a number of topics have been expanded or clarified. We also believe that the book organizes and presents the discussion in a more useful fashion.

We still do not select a "preferred" method, although it will be clear that in our view, obtaining an accurate estimate of the cost of capital is far more difficult for some methods than others. We do attempt to distinguish our opinions from the findings of financial research, and we provide citations to the latter when such findings must be cited without detailed justification.

This book is intended to serve both regulatory practitioners and students of regulation as an introduction to determining the cost of capital and as a reference. This is a field characterized by conflicting claims and strongly held views. If we are successful, those who must evaluate the claims of contending analysts will find their task easier, and those who disagree will find their differences more clearly defined.

Acknowledgments

This book owes an enormous debt to Stewart Myers of the Sloan School of Management, MIT. Professor Myers worked actively on the original project for the California Public Utilities Commission (CPUC) and was a principal author of the resulting report. He also was a member of the workshop faculty for the project. Beyond his direct participation in that project, the authors of this book have benefited greatly from their work with him over a period of years, and he offered very helpful suggestions on how this book might be organized and prepared. If his schedule had permitted, he would clearly be one of the book's authors; as it is, he deserves much of the credit but none of the responsibility for any shortcomings.

The other members of the CPUC project team were Robert Lincoln and Carin Boyer. They did not participate in turning the project report into this book, but both have our thanks for their contributions to the original effort and their indirect contribution to this book. We also thank John Bryson, then President of the CPUC, for his encouragement and help in shaping the overall direction of that project, and the staff of the CPUC who worked with us directly, including James Pretti, Terry Mowrey, Cathy Waddell, and Duncan Wyse. We are likewise indebted to Gerald Pogue of Baruch College, CUNY. Professor Pogue made the empirical comparisons of chapter 4 possible by sharing with us data that he had created for his own research during the original project for the CPUC.

Finally, we wish to thank Ruth Kolbe for her encouragement and for putting up with the hours we spent on nights and weekends to meet the publishing deadline. We couldn't have done it without you.

A. Lawrence Kolbe
James A. Read, Jr.
George R. Hall

The Cost of Capital

1 The Setting: Utility Regulation and Capital Markets

What are society's alternatives when faced with a natural monopoly, as in the distribution of electric power? It can do nothing and accept whatever market structure arises. It can establish a government enterprise to provide the monopoly services. Or it can allow business to operate subject to regulation by a government agency. The first alternative has generally been rejected on the grounds that the consequences of permitting an unrestrained monopoly are unacceptable. Government ownership of public utilities exists in the United States (usually at the state or local level) and is common in other countries. The third alternative, however, the investor-owned utility regulated by a state commission, is the predominant form of organization in this country.

While this form limits the exercise of monopoly power, it raises many practical and conceptual questions. What goals should the regulatory agency adopt? What are the best ways to accomplish these goals? When the goals conflict, what are the consequences of different compromises? The study of such questions is a field encompassing several disciplines (law, economics, finance and accounting) and a long history of research. A multitude of public-policy issues confronts utility regulation and those who study it today—energy price shocks, full or partial deregulation in some industries, environmental problems, high interest rates, construction delays, and cost overruns—but we are concerned here with only one, which comes down to a basic and practical issue of measurement.

This book is a tool to deal with the problems created by the profusion of new methods to answer one of the most controversial questions in utility regulation: What is the "fair" rate of return to allow to utility investors? This question is of practical interest in every utility rate hearing and to every customer who complains about utility rates and every investor who sees his or her utility stock fall in value when interest rates rise.

Answers can come from several places. The law looks to the decisions of the Supreme Court. We look chiefly to the principles of financial economics, or "finance." Finance provides a framework for defining in principle the appropriate rate of return for an investor-owned utility. Analytical techniques based on the concepts of finance provide ways to estimate this rate of return in practice. The last twenty years have brought important strides in our understanding of capital markets and finance. Although finance theory is far from complete, one can say much more today than in the past about the return a utility's investors should receive for the risks they bear.

From the regulators' perspective this is not necessarily a blessing. While the theory and practice of finance continue to yield new insights for regulation, the requisite technical background is expanding and increasing in sophistication, placing ever greater demands on those who wish to understand these developments. To make matters worse, no sooner is one supposed improvement incorporated into regulatory practice than another "expert" comes along with something entirely new. If an already overburdened regulatory system cannot sift through new methods and procedures and, when appropriate, modify or abandon the old, outworn procedures may persist long past the time for their retirement.

This book aims to reduce the burden for regulatory practitioners and to introduce the relevant issues to students of regulation. It is not a substitute for a textbook in finance. Our focus is on the identification of the "fair" rate of return for the regulated company in principle, the examination of the available techniques for estimating it in practice, and the exploration of the assumptions underlying these techniques.

1. Problems Facing Utility Regulation

Most regulators seem to feel that the chief goal of utility regulation is to protect the customers' interests. From this perspective the concern with a "fair" return to investors must balance two needs: customers should not be overcharged for the capital investors supply, and investors must be paid enough to assure that the requisite capital will be available to meet customers' needs in the future.

The difficulties of achieving this balance have not resulted merely from a plethora of ways to estimate the required rate of return (although after chapter 2, we will be speaking as though such difficulties arose only because of technical estimation problems). Discrepancies between the rate of return that regulators allow and the rate that finance would label "fair" also arise because of more fundamental problems facing utility regulation.

During the 1970s the economic climate for industries subject to rate regulation changed significantly. All were affected by the increase in the level and volatility of inflation.[1] Many (the electric utility industry in particular) were hurt by dramatic increases in the cost of petroleum and other energy resources, by more stringent environmental and safety standards, and by increased construction costs. The results have included higher costs for ratepayers, reduced rates of industry growth, and financial difficulties for a number of regulated firms. Public utility rate hearings are more frequent and more contentious than in earlier, quieter times.

Currently, at least four alleged problems are major topics of discussion in regulatory circles.

1. Some expenses are incurred by utility companies but never recovered in utility rates. Examples include cancelled plants, other charges disallowed as not prudently incurred, or cost increases that occur between the date of filing and the date of approval for a rate increase, at least in some jurisdictions.

2. Some items are alleged to be improperly included or excluded (depending on the jurisdiction and the perspective of the individual making the point) from the amount of capital used to provide service. Examples include construction work in progress (CWIP) and abandoned plants.

3. Companies sometimes show a sustained inability to achieve the allowed rate of return. This is commonly referred to as the "earnings attrition" problem.

4. Regulators are accused of failing to set utility rates high enough to reflect the "true" costs of service. One of the most important elements of the cost of service is the allowed return on investment, which is sometimes said to fall short of the true cost of capital.[2]

This book addresses issues in the last area, in particular how the cost of capital can be estimated.

A number of the remedies proposed for these problems aim at

improving the existing regulatory framework. Some observers advocate making rate increases automatic when the rate of return on equity falls below a target level, a procedure similar to the fuel-adjustment clause. The target rate of return must be reset in a regulatory hearing when capital market conditions change, but investors are less exposed to loss in the period of regulatory lag between hearings.[3]

Others advocate indexing the allowed rate of return on equity to the interest rate on bonds, so that the rate of return can be adjusted without the need for new rate-of-return testimony each time capital market conditions change.[4]

Some suggest changing the methodology used to value the utility rate base so that investors are compensated for inflation through capital gains rather than current earnings. This would stabilize utility rates when the rate of inflation is in flux and lessen the need for frequent hearings. It would also reduce the difficulties commissions have in trying to recognize simultaneously the legitimate interests of investors and ratepayers.[5]

Still other proposals are aimed at deregulation of industry rather than regulatory reform. Substantial deregulation of parts of the natural gas industry and of the commercial aviation, motor freight, and telecommunications industries has occurred already. Deregulation of electricity generation has been proposed.[6]

If proponents are correct, some of these procedural and substantive reforms would speed up regulation and address the alleged problems more directly than would an improved method of estimating the required rate of return on equity. Some reforms, such as deregulation, would eliminate the need to estimate the cost of capital altogether, at least in some contexts. This book assumes continuation of the present system of public utility regulation and addresses how one aspect of that system can be improved.

A growing body of expert testimony claims to offer methods of estimating the cost of capital superior to those used traditionally—some of which are still prevalent. Changes in the way capital markets seem to behave in times of high and volatile rates of inflation (and the financial problems facing many regulated companies) lend credence to the argument that traditional methods need to be refined or replaced.

Our aim is not to select a "preferred" method of rate-of-return estimation but to offer students of regulation, regulatory commissions and their staffs, utility managers, and investors a clear explanation of the various techniques and a balanced description of their relative advantages and disadvantages.

2. The Ratemaking Process

At this point it will be helpful to review the institutional setting in which the fair rate of return is debated. The process usually begins with a formal request by a public utility for a change in rates, accompanied by submission of evidence in support of the request. The regulatory commission under whose jurisdiction this utility falls presides over a formal proceeding in which this evidence, along with evidence submitted by other parties (commission staff, customers, and others) is presented and examined.

The requested rate increase is justified by demonstrating an increase in costs. The governing principle is that customers should pay the cost, but no more than the cost, of providing the services they use. The sum of all the approved costs of service is called the "revenue requirement." One of the elements of cost is the return the company's investors receive for supplying capital. Utility rates are then set to generate an amount of revenue equal to the revenue requirement at the expected level of demand for each service. In some transportation industries, revenue requirements have traditionally been set for a group of companies rather than for each company separately.

Different procedures are used by different regulatory commissions to estimate the costs and levels of service. Some base their estimates on costs in historical test years; others use forecasts of costs in the future. Many commissions allow automatic rate adjustments for cost items too volatile to be left fixed between ratemaking hearings (the most common adjustments are for fuel costs).

Conditions may change during the period the new rates are in effect. The usual regulatory practice and legal precedent preclude "retroactive ratemaking"—going back and changing past rates to reflect actual costs. The customer must know in advance what the product or service will cost; also, retroactive ratemaking can create perverse incentives for managers. Consequently, the regulated company may earn more or less than the allowed rate of return on equity while the rates are in effect, depending in part on the accuracy of the forecasts used to set rates and in part on unforeseen developments. Hence the term *allowed* rather than *guaranteed* rate of return. If rates do not yield an acceptable rate of return, the utility must file a new rate case or the utility commission must take action on its own to set a new rate.

There is often a period of notice before new rates can go into effect. In addition many commissions have the authority to suspend rates for some specified period before they take effect. If higher costs do justify the rate increase as of the filing date, the notice and suspension periods prevent recovery of these higher costs because of the prohibition against retroactive ratemaking. Several approaches exist to try to deal with this problem.

Some jurisdictions permit rates to go into effect under bond or subject to refund. In these jurisdictions, the utility may file a new rate case prior to the final decision on the old rate by the commission. The new rate filing "locks in" the old rate. In other words, the commission's decision on the first case then deals with a historic period and has no prospective application. The new rate filing establishes a new rate level (also subject to refund), which will remain in effect even if the decision on the first case is that a refund is appropriate. A series of rate filings all awaiting final action is said to be "pancaking" of rates.

Other jurisdictions do not permit rates to be in effect subject to refund. In such cases, locked-in periods and pancaking are not problems, but there is much pressure for early action on filings. The trouble is that utilities can never recover the difference between the old "just and reasonable" rates and the higher costs (used to justify the new rates) it incurs while waiting for the new rates to be approved. Some commissions address these problems by standardizing rate hearings on a fixed cycle. The rates corresponding to the expected costs always go into effect on the first day of the next period in the cycle.

The chief task of the ratemaking proceeding is to estimate as precisely as possible the costs of providing service given the expected demand for service. On the basis of estimated costs and demand, rates are set that will just recover the cost of the service if the expected level of service is provided.

The allowance made for a number of costs is subject to controversy. For example, taxes are allowed as a cost of service. Commissions have varied considerably in their treatment of the way tax expense is computed, with debate focused principally on treatment of the effects of accelerated depreciation for federal income tax computation.[7] A commission may sometimes decide that an expense is not a legitimate cost of service and refuse to include an allowance for it in the revenue requirement.

One of the most controversial elements of the ratemaking process is the rate of return allowed on invested capital. The amount of capital used to provide service is called the "rate base." In recent decades, the value of the rate base has been relatively uncontroversial, although debates persist over exactly what items should be included. The debate now centers on the rate of return to be allowed on the rate base. Understanding the debate requires an understanding of capital and capital markets.

3. Capital and Capital Markets in Ratemaking

The word *capital* has two meanings. It may refer to real assets—property, plant, and equipment—used in the production of goods and services. Or it may refer to the monetary assets used to purchase these real assets. In the first case we speak of "physical capital" or "capital goods" and in the second case of "financial capital."

Financial capital is used to purchase the capital goods and the working capital[8] required to produce goods or services. It is provided by investors in exchange for securities (stocks and bonds) issued by a corporation. Securities are legal claims to the assets and future earnings of a corporation. Thus capital markets are an interface between investors and corporations.

In most jurisdictions, the largest part of the utility rate base is the original cost of utility plant, less accumulated depreciation. Other jurisdictions compute the "fair value" of the utility plant, using a variety of methods that are sometimes poorly understood outside the commission.

Physical capital is an asset of a corporation; financial capital is a liability. On a corporate balance sheet, physical and net working capital are assets and financial capital (debt and equity) is a liability. Since total assets and total liabilities are equal, the rate base can be viewed in terms of assets—plant and equipment—or liabilities—debt and equity. Investors expect a return on the capital they provide; the amount of this return over a given period divided by the initial value of the investment is the rate of return. The return on the rate base is compensation paid to utility investors for the capital they have provided.

Securities are traded in capital markets (for example, the New York

Stock Exchange), where competition among securities offering different expected returns and having different risks sets the price for each. Depending on the context, "market" value refers either to the current price of the security in capital markets (the price of one share of common stock) or to the aggregate value at the current price of all of a company's securities of this type (the price per share times the number of shares outstanding).

The return investors expect when buying a security consists of two components. One component is the cash distribution; interest in the case of bonds and dividends in the case of stock. The other is price appreciation, often referred to as capital gains. The sum of cash distributions and capital gains is the total return on investment.

To attract investment capital a regulated company must offer investors the prospect of a return comparable to that expected from alternative investments. The difficulty in measuring this comparable return is that the expectations of equity investors are not directly observable. Unlike the price of other resources that a utility purchases, the price of risk capital is not posted. But various methods have evolved to infer the unobservable rates of return investors expect.

Once an approved rate of return on equity and the other cost estimates are available, the revenue requirement can be computed. The rate base is divided into parts that reflect the share of the capital supplied by different types of investors, as recorded on the company's books. For example, if the balance sheet showed 40 percent of the company had been financed by debt and 60 percent by equity, the equity share of the rate base would be set at 60 percent. (There may also be other securities, such as preferred stock.)

The overall return on capital can be computed in two ways. The allowed rate of return on equity can be multiplied by the equity share of the rate base to compute the allowed return on equity (the after-tax income) to be included in the revenue requirement. Actual interest expense is added to this amount to get the total return on capital.[9]

The second method multiplies the allowed rate of return on equity by the equity share of the rate base. The average rate of interest on the company's outstanding debt (known as the "embedded" cost of debt) is multiplied by the debt share of the rate base. The two values are added to get the "weighted average cost of capital."[10] This value multiplied by the value of the rate base gives the total return on capital.

In either case, the commission-approved tax expenses that correspond to the allowed level of after-tax income are added to the other estimated expenses and to the total return allowed investors to get the total revenue requirement. The forecasts of the quantities to be sold to the various customer classes are used to set rates that are expected to recover this revenue requirement. (Fixing the structure of rates for different service classes is in itself a complex subject and is not addressed in this book.)

4. Plan of the Book

Our discussion has implicitly assumed that regulators should seek to equate the cost of capital prevailing in financial markets and the rate of return allowed to a utility's stockholders. Why do we make this assumption? Many people doubt or actively dispute the appropriateness of this policy. Yet, if the reader does not accept this fundamental premise, our evaluation standards will make no sense and this book will be of little value.

For this reason, chapter 2 explores the proposition in depth. We first define the cost of capital and then explain why the allowed rate of return should be equal to the cost of capital from the standpoints of law, economics, and what for want of a better word we call "fairness." Chapter 2 also reviews the rationale for a policy recommendation often made to regulators: try to set the allowed rate of return so the market value of the firm's stock will equal the book value of the physical assets it represents. This turns out to be simply another way of saying that the allowed rate of return should be set equal to the cost of capital. However, approaching the premise from this direction yields important additional insights into why such a policy is "fair" to all parties. Finally, chapter 2 reviews the consequences of failure to equate the allowed rate of return and the cost of capital, in the process addressing some of the reasons that such failures have been frequent in the last decade.

Chapter 3 turns to the criteria we use to evaluate the cost-of-capital estimation methods. These standards are classified as: theoretical (the assumptions needed, logical consistency, and consistency with the current understanding of how capital markets work); practical (the time and resources needed); and empirical (how well the method seems to work in actual applications).

After the exposition of evaluation criteria, we turn to a formal evaluation of the five major methods: Comparable Earnings, Discounted Cash Flow, Capital Asset Pricing Model, Risk Positioning, and Market-to-Book Ratio. For each method in turn, we state the method's definition and assumptions and provide a simplified numerical example; examine its logical consistency and its consistency with current theory; and consider its data requirements and review the associated administrative and related costs. We then summarize the implications of the conceptual evaluation for all five methods.

Chapter 4 completes the evaluation of the five major methods and summarizes each method's performance with respect to the criteria defined in chapter 3. To conduct the empirical review, we select standard procedures that can be easily applied to each method. While actual applications of the various methods are often more sophisticated, the choice of which more sophisticated variation to employ requires a substantial dollop of "expert judgment." Our view is that the empirical review is more useful if it concentrates on the basic technique simply applied, so that readers get a better feel for how well the starting point of any sophisticated variation performs, and for how important it is likely to be to make some adjustment to the basic approach.

We have separated the empirical work in chapter 4 from the conceptual review in chapter 3 for two reasons. Because most of the empirical tests apply to several methods, comparing results would be difficult if they were reported separately for the individual methods. Second, two of the methods (Risk Positioning and Market-to-Book Ratio) are not as precisely defined as the others. They lack a widely agreed upon basic technique, and any simple approach we selected for comparison could correctly be labeled nonrepresentative.

Chapter 5 looks ahead at methods that may become more important in the future. One problem facing regulatory practitioners is keeping up with a rapidly evolving body of theory and practice. While we cannot be sure that our predictions of future developments will be borne out, we believe it will be useful for many readers to have a preview of what may be coming, both for its own sake and to help place existing methods in context.

In addition to the main text, there are three appendixes. Appendix A shows how the proportion of debt in a company's capital structure affects the cost of equity. This topic is too often overlooked when comparing the costs of equity of different companies or when considering the overall cost of capital that would exist if a particular company had a different debt-equity ratio. While peripheral to the main concerns of the book, the issues in appendix A are vital to correct estimation of the cost of equity when variations in the debt-equity ratio exist.

Appendix B discusses an offshoot of the market-to-book test of whether a company is expected to earn its cost of equity. Specifically, it uses the concept of vintaged equity returns to further illustrate the nature of the market-to-book test. Finally, appendix C contains the technical notes on the empirical analysis of chapter 4.

2 The Cost of Capital: What It Is and Why It Matters

Why should the cost of capital "set on Wall Street" determine the rate of return that a utility thousands of miles away should receive? This chapter provides the answer. It defines the cost of capital and then shows why the cost of capital is the right target for the allowed rate of return.

1. The Concept of the Cost of Capital

The cost of capital is the minimum rate of return necessary to attract capital to an investment.[1] It can be defined as "the expected rate of return prevailing in capital markets on alternative investments of equivalent risk." There are four ideas contained in this definition:

1. The cost of capital is a forward-looking concept. Investment returns are inherently uncertain; actual returns may differ from expected returns. The cost of capital is an *expected* rate of return.
2. The cost of capital is an *opportunity cost* concept. Investors face a variety of investment opportunities, so the expected rate of return on any investment must be sufficient to compensate investors for the expected rate of return on foregone investments.
3. The cost of capital is determined in *capital markets.* It is a market price expressed in terms of the expected return per dollar invested. This market price establishes a balance between the supply of and the demand for capital.
4. The cost of capital depends on the *risk* of the investment.[2] It is the expected rate of return on investments of equivalent risk. Put another way, it is the rate of return that investors could expect to earn on other investments while bearing no more and no less risk.

The cost of capital is sometimes referred to as "the opportunity cost of capital" or " the required rate of return." Both phrases convey the idea that alternative investment opportunities provide a frame of reference for the cost of capital.

This definition implies that the cost of capital depends on the risk of the investment, not on the specific individual or firm undertaking it. This principle is often expressed by saying that the cost of capital depends on the *use* of funds, not on the *source*.[3] Thus, a risky company should not require a high rate of return to engage in riskless investments. Conversely, a low-risk company should demand a high rate of return on a high-risk investment. Prudent managers evaluate each potential investment on its merits and accept it only if the expected return justifies the risk.

Because the cost of capital depends on the use of funds, it is important to distinguish between the cost of capital for a company and the cost of capital for an investment. A company can be thought of as a collection of investments. The cost of capital for a company is a weighted average of the costs of capital for the various investments of which the company is comprised. Thus the cost of capital for a company is not necessarily equal to the cost of capital for an investment owned by the company. Moreover, it is not necessarily equal to the cost of capital for an investment the company may make in the future.

Relationship among Costs of Capital for Different Investments

Investors are generally risk averse: more risky investments must offer higher expected returns than less risky ones in order to attract capital. This fact of life constrains those trying to finance capital investment.

The active, competitive nature of capital markets leads to a direct relationship between the degree of risk perceived by investors and the expected return investments must offer to induce investors to bear that risk. The relationship between risk and the required rate of return is often termed the "market risk-return line" (the "market line" for short). Figure 2.1 shows the relationship between risk and the cost of capital, $\bar{r}$, in "nominal" (current dollar) terms. The intercept of the risk-return line is the risk-free rate of interest, r_f. In academic studies, r_f is usually measured by the rate of return on U.S. Treasury bills. This return is riskless in the sense that the amount and timing of a bill's cash payoff are known exactly. The likelihood of a United States government default is negligible.[4]

Figure 2.2 expresses the market line in real terms. Inflation is "backed out" of the nominal rates of return by subtracting an inflation premium. The inflation premium equals the rate of inflation forecasted by investors. For example, if the expected rate of inflation is 10

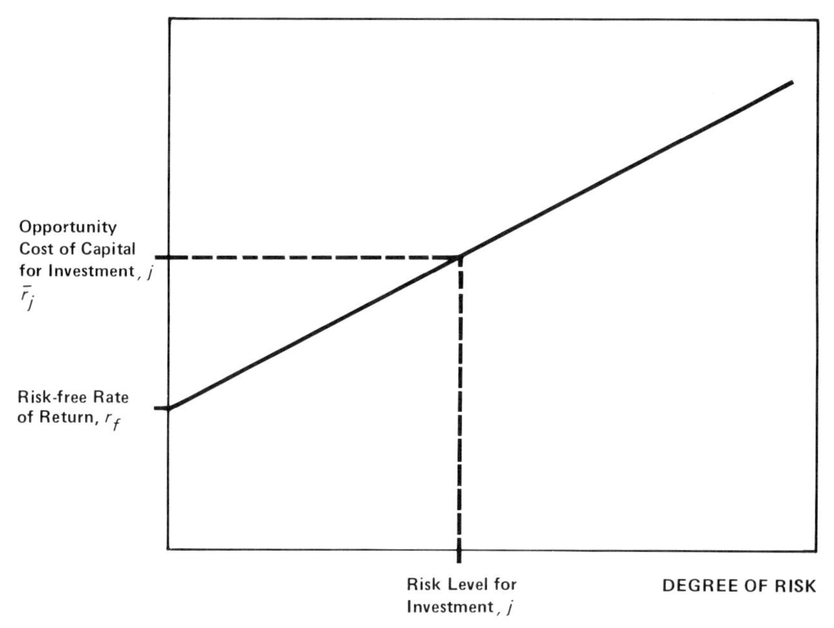

Figure 2.1
The Risk-Return Trade-Off in Capital Markets

percent, real costs of capital lie ten percentage points below nominal costs of capital at every level of risk.

Many events can lead to a change in the cost of capital for a company. These events may be specific to the company or common to the economy as a whole. The addition of a new line of business or a change in corporate financial policy are events specific to a company; an increase in the expected rate of inflation is an event common to the economy. The distinction between these kinds of events is important for estimating the cost of capital.

This distinction is illustrated in figure 2.3. If the company becomes riskier, the cost of capital for the company increases even if the rest of the market is unaffected. If the entire market line shifts up (because, for example, the expected rate of inflation increases), the company's nominal cost of capital increases even if the company itself is no more or less risky than before.

Some factors shifting the market line might change its slope as well as its intercept, but identifying such factors and quantifying their effects is very difficult. (Such factors must somehow change the risk

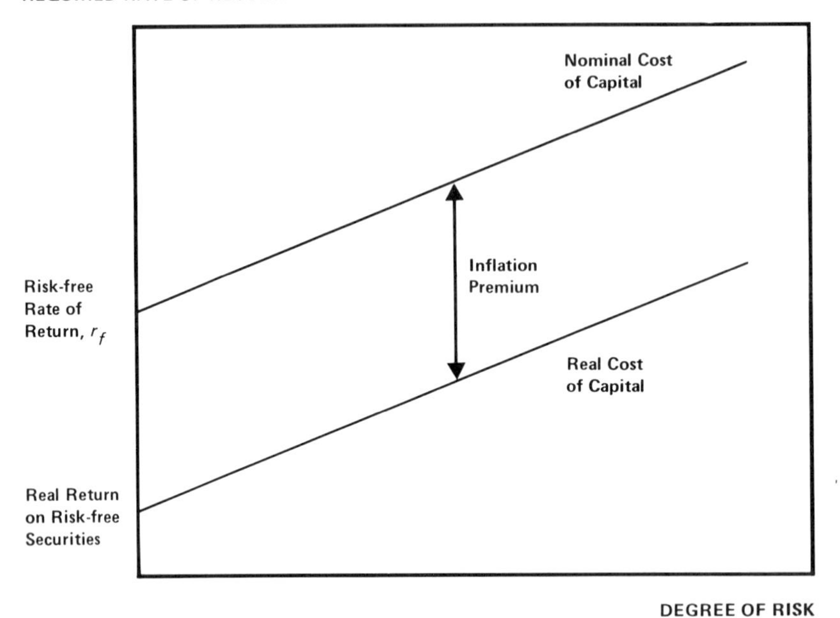

Figure 2.2
The Inflation-Adjusted Risk-Return Trade-Off

premium that investors demand for the average financial asset.) In our view, since changes in the slope of the line are as likely to be up as down, the most reasonable approach in the regulatory setting usually will be to assume parallel shifts in the market line.[5]

The Impact of Debt on the Cost of Equity Capital

Investors are exposed to two kinds of risk when they own a share of common stock. There is the risk inherent in the operations of the corporation because of uncertainty about future earnings and asset values, and there is an additional risk introduced by corporate borrowing. We refer to the first as "business risk" and the second as "financial risk." If a company is financed entirely by equity capital, then stockholders are exposed only to business risk. If a company meets a portion of its capital requirements through debt financing, then stockholders bear both business and financial risk.

The priority of claims is central to financial risk. Lenders have first

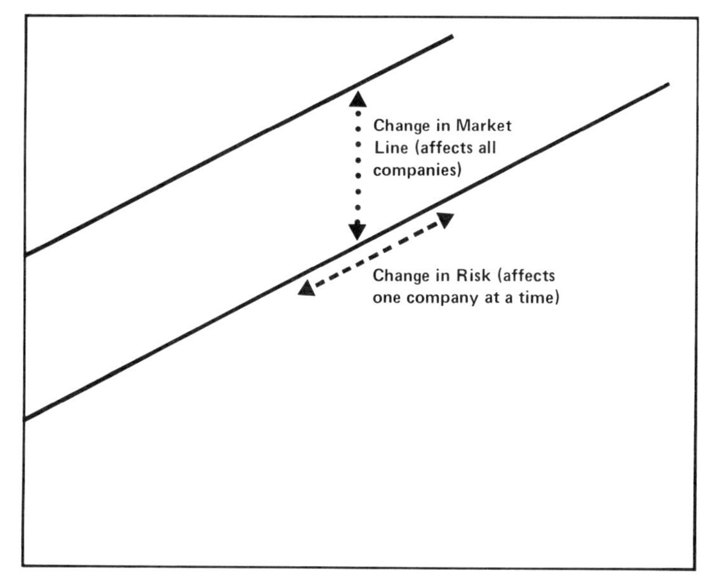

Figure 2.3
Changes in the Required Rate of Return

claim to the operating earnings of the corporation and, in the event of bankruptcy, first claim on assets. The stockholders' claim is to the residual of earnings and assets. Interest expense is a fixed cost for a corporation that borrows. Although earnings are reduced by interest expense, they are allocated to a smaller equity base since there is less equity capital in a corporation that borrows. Thus debt finance is said to "leverage" the risk and return of common stock.

One implication of the market risk-return relationship is that the additional risk to investors who hold shares of leveraged companies must be offset by higher expected returns. Financial leverage increases the cost of equity capital. This can be interpreted by means of the market line. If two firms have the same business risk but one borrows more than the other, the leveraged firm will lie farther to the right on the market line and will have a higher cost of equity capital.

The mix of debt and equity capital in corporate finance is referred to as "capital structure." Capital structure is usually summarized by reference to the debt-equity ratio—the ratio of debt capital to equity capital—or to the debt ratio—the ratio of debt to total capitalization. A corporation financed one half by debt and one half by equity would have a debt-equity ratio equal to 1.0 and a debt ratio equal to 0.5.

Unfortunately, the relationship between capital structure and the cost of capital is not fully understood. The central issue is how the cost of capital is influenced by the differential tax treatment of debt and equity. Two polar positions can be identified.

One position is that the firm's overall cost of capital (the combined cost of the firm's debt and equity) is reduced by corporate borrowing, because interest is a deductible expense for corporate tax purposes. A dollar paid out as interest expense reduces after-tax income, but only by a fraction of a dollar. Thus, substituting debt capital for equity capital tends to reduce the tax liability of the corporation and to increase the total amount of funds available for payment to investors, which, in this view, lowers the overall cost of funds.

The opposing position holds that cost of capital is unaffected by corporate borrowing; capital structure does not matter. This argument recognizes that while the corporate tax code favors debt finance, the personal tax code favors equity finance. The return on corporate bonds comes mainly in the form of interest payments, which are taxed at the personal income tax rate. The return to common stocks, in contrast, comes mainly in the form of capital gains, which are taxed at the lower capital gains rate. Moreover, the tax on capital gains is deferred until the shares are traded. Thus, the second view is that the corporate tax benefit of debt finance is offset by the personal tax benefit of equity finance.

Each position can be summarized by two equations, one relating the overall cost of capital to financial leverage and the other relating the cost of equity capital to financial leverage. Let r denote the overall cost of capital, r_e the cost of equity capital, and r_d the cost of debt capital; let t denote the tax rate, D the value of debt, and E the value of equity. Then if the first position is correct, these equations hold:

$$r = \left[(1 - t)\left(\frac{D}{D + E}\right) \times r_d\right] + \left[\left(\frac{E}{D + E}\right) \times r_e\right],$$

$$r_e = r + (1 - t)\,(r - r_d)\,\frac{D}{E}.$$

If the second position is correct, that is if capital structure does not matter, then these alternative equations hold:[6]

$$r = \left[\left(\frac{D}{D + E}\right) \times r_d\right] + \left[\left(\frac{E}{D + E}\right) \times r_e\right]$$

$$r_e = r + (r - r_d)\frac{D}{E}.$$

The subject of capital structure is a good deal more complicated than this review suggests. Appendix A contains a more thorough discussion of the relationship between capital structure and the cost of capital. Our view is that the answer lies somewhere between these two extreme positions. There is probably some advantage to modest levels of debt finance but, for a variety of reasons, this advantage is eroded as leverage increases.

Why is the effect of leverage on the cost of equity capital important? First, the leverage of a company rarely stays constant; if one wants to use historical evidence to infer the cost of equity capital, correction for changes in leverage may be necessary. Second, evidence for other companies is often used to infer the cost of equity capital, and these companies may be subject to more or less financial risk than the company under study. Adjustments to their estimated costs of equity will usually be necessary to avoid an "apples and oranges" comparison.

Our objective is to evaluate methods used to estimate the cost of equity capital. Henceforth, we will use "cost of capital" to mean the cost of equity capital. And when we use the word *risk,* we will not distinguish between business risk and financial risk.

Strategies for Cost of Capital Estimation

In sum, the cost of equity capital depends on the risk of the investment, the risks and returns on alternative investments, and on capital structure and its effect on risk. These forces underlie the market line, which relates the required rate of return to risk. Given this framework, the methods used to estimate the cost of capital for regulatory hearings can take one of two basic strategies. They can estimate the cost of capital directly, or assess the stock's risk first, then estimate the required rate of return for that degree of risk.

To estimate the firm's cost of capital directly, the analyst examines evidence on the rates of return already earned or anticipated in the future for investments believed to be of the same risk as the firm. Methods taking this direct approach include Comparable Earnings and Discounted Cash Flow (the techniques mentioned here are defined and evaluated in chapter 3). Since these methods look only at firms in a single "risk class," they do not require that the analyst estimate the entire risk-return line shown in figure 2.1; they focus directly on the vertical axis.

To use the second strategy, the analyst must examine (at least implicitly) both measures of the stock's risk and the current position of the market line. Methods that require explicit risk measurement include the Capital Asset Pricing Model and the Risk Positioning techniques. These methods first position the firm on the horizontal axis of figure 2.1, and then (again, at least implicitly) use an estimate of the risk-return line to find the proper level for the cost of capital on the vertical axis.

The advantages of one strategy are the disadvantages of the other. The first strategy avoids the need for an estimate of the market line but requires that the evidence used must be from investments of comparable risk. This immediately excludes data from other firms of differing risk. More subtly, it can exclude data on the firm whose cost of capital is now being estimated, if either its risk or the market line has changed since the evidence was collected.

This focus on estimation strategies may be premature. If the reader does not accept that the cost of capital as just defined is the right target for regulators, the general approaches to cost of capital estimation may be of little interest. The remainder of the chapter uses two approaches to develop the reasons that the cost of capital is indeed the appropriate allowed rate of return for a regulated company's investors.[7]

2. Why the Allowed Rate of Return Should Equal the Cost of Capital

Law

The United States Supreme Court has established that investors in companies subject to rate regulation must be allowed *an opportunity* to earn returns sufficient to attract capital and comparable to those they would expect in the unregulated sector for bearing the same degree of risk. The *Bluefield* and *Hope* cases provide the seminal decisions.[8]

The *Hope* test is the basic criterion for a legally sufficient rate of return on equity. The court stated:

> The rate-making process under the act, i.e., the fixing of "just and reasonable" rates, involves a balancing of the investor and the consumer interests. Thus we stated in the *Natural Gas Pipeline Co.* case that "regulation does not insure that the business shall produce net revenues." 315 U.S. p. 590. But such considerations aside, the investor interest has a legitimate concern with the financial integrity of the company whose rates are being regulated. From the investor or company point of view it is important that there be enough revenue not only for operating expenses but also for the capital costs of the business. These include service on the debt and dividends on the stock . . . . By that standard the return to the equity owner should be commensurate with returns on investments in other enterprises having corresponding risks. That return, moreover, should be sufficient to assure confidence in the financial integrity of the enterprise, so as to maintain its credit and to attract capital.[9]

Since by definition the cost of capital of a regulated firm represents precisely the expected return that investors could anticipate from other investments while bearing no more and no less risk, and since investors will not provide capital unless the investment is expected to yield its opportunity cost of capital, the correspondence of the definition of the cost of capital with the court's definition of legally required earnings appears clear. *Hope* refers to both "commensurate" earnings and the attraction of capital. These two approaches are harmonized when the allowed rate of return is set equal to the cost of capital.

Hope is sometimes cited for the proposition that some specific method of establishing the rate of return on equity is the only legally permissible technique. However, *Hope* states clearly that it is the "end result" of the regulation process that determines legality, not the specific technique used to calculate rate of return. All the standard cost-of-capital estimation techniques can meet the requisite legal tests; it is the way they are applied that is important.

Despite the obvious correspondence between the precepts of *Hope* and the financial concept of the cost of capital, public utility statutes and the applicable case law give no detailed prescription for what constitutes a "just and reasonable" rate of return on equity. In the absence of detailed guidelines from legislatures or the higher courts, various general judicial concepts about rate setting have been developed and applied by courts. The key concepts are:

1. Balance: the establishment of a just and reasonable rate involves a balancing of the investor and consumer interests.

2. Zone of reasonableness: the lawful, just, and reasonable rate is not a "point" figure. Instead, the law envisions a zone within which the allowed rate of return determined by a commission must fall.[10]

3. Discretion: public utility commissions have broad discretion in setting rates of return within the zone of reasonableness, since their function is primarily "legislative" rather than "judicial."[11]

The discretion of commissions is limited in some respects. Specifically, a lawful rate cannot be set so low as to be "confiscatory";[12] nor can it be set so high as to provide "excessive" returns to investors.[13] But no case law defines with precision "confiscatory" or "excessive." The discretion of public utility commissions is also limited by the requirement of meeting procedural standards. The ratesetting process must be fair and orderly, and provide an adequate decisional record.[14]

The applicable legal standards permit public utility commissions to choose among a variety of analytical techniques and procedures in setting the allowed rate of return on equity. On the other hand, a conscious effort to equate the allowed rate of return with the cost of capital makes it easy to demonstrate that the designated rate is within the zone of reasonableness and is a lawful, just, and reasonable rate.

Economics

Direct and indirect economic benefits flow from setting the allowed rate of return for a regulated firm equal to the cost of capital. The direct benefits are that the firm's customers will pay the lowest cost for service in the long run if the firm's investors expect the allowed rate of return to equal the cost of capital. The indirect benefits are an assurance that society's supply of capital will be used where it is most productive.

To understand the direct benefits, suppose that regulators set the rate of return above the cost of capital. Then stockholders will earn more than they could elsewhere on comparable-risk investments. Customers pay for this extra return, but could receive the same service without paying the extra amount.

Conversely, if regulators set the rate of return below the cost of capital, stockholders earn less than they could elsewhere on comparable-risk investments. While today's customers may gain from this policy, tomorrow's customers are likely to lose. Managers will recognize that they are penalizing stockholders whenever they make a new investment, because the expected return will fall short of the cost of capital. Managers will grow increasingly unwilling to add to existing capacity.[15]

If these conditions persist long enough, customers will have to make do with less efficient equipment (for example, from failure to replace oil-fired electricity generating stations), and with less capacity and a lower safety margin (as indicated by more frequent service outages). Although less easily quantified, inferior service is as much a cost to customers as excessive rates.

The indirect benefits of equating the allowed return and the cost of capital arise because capital markets are highly competitive, which implies that the cost of new capital is a good measure of the value of that capital in alternative uses. If the allowed rate of return exceeds the cost of capital, investors have an artificial incentive to use capital in the regulated industry. Capital may be bid away from alternative investments where it would be more productive.[16] Conversely, if the allowed rate of return falls short of the cost of capital, capital that should have been used in the regulated sector may be used elsewhere in a less productive investment. Society as a whole suffers from this misallocation of scarce resources.

There is another way to state the economic argument for using the cost of capital as a profitability standard for regulated firms. Regulation is a substitute for the discipline of competitive markets. Ideal regulation would induce the firm to act as if it faced a competitive industry. A competitive firm invests up to the point where the expected rate of return on investment equals the cost of capital. A commission that reduces allowed rates of return when the firm is earning more than its cost of capital and increases allowed rates when the firm is earning less simulates competition. If it succeeds, it provides the benefits of competition, namely: a cost to consumers that covers only the true cost of providing the product or service; and an efficient allocation of capital between regulated and unregulated industry.

Fairness

Deciding what is "fair" (or "just" or "equitable") is an essential but extremely difficult element of a regulator's job. There is no simple, obvious definition of "fair," which is one reason regulatory commissions exist. But setting the allowed rate of return equal to the cost of capital satisfies the usual notions of regulatory fairness.

One underlying premise of cost-based regulation is that customers should pay the cost of providing the service they get. The cost of most factors used to provide the service is readily observable (wages, fuel costs, and so forth). Equity capital is a factor that must be paid for like any of the others, but its cost is hard to measure. Despite the difficulty of measuring this cost exactly, for consumers not to pay it would be as unfair as not paying a laborer the wage for which he or she agreed to work. The cost of equity capital is precisely the foregone rate of return on a comparably risky investment. Therefore, setting the allowed rate of return equal to this cost is "fair" to investors.

Another premise of regulation is that customers should be protected from the exercise of the potential monopoly power that may exist in the industries society chooses to regulate. One undesirable consequence of monopoly power is the earning of excess returns on investment. But "excess" returns must be defined with respect to some standard, and in economics this standard is the rate of return that would be required on this investment by a competitive industry—the cost of capital. This is the return the investor could earn elsewhere, in an unregulated industry of comparable risk. Setting the allowed rate of return equal to the cost of capital avoids excess returns and is "fair" to customers.[17]

Of course, there may be other definitions of fairness. One notion is that any contract for which all parties understand the terms is fair if arrived at freely. Explicit or implicit contracts among regulators, customers, and investors that require allowed rates of return *not* equal to the cost of capital could still be fair, providing all parties understood in advance that this was a condition of the contract.

For example, suppose regulators consciously respond to rapid changes in the cost of capital with a lag, to avoid increasing the costs to customers too quickly when the cost of capital goes up. To be fair to investors, the lag in response would have to be equally long when the cost of capital declines, and the full increase sooner or later would have to be recognized in allowed rates of return in some fashion.[18]

However, this procedure risks introducing many of the economic costs of failing to set the allowed rate of return equal to the cost of capital, especially if investors were not confident that the bargain would be honored on the downside as well as the up. There is also a question of which customers benefit and which investors pay. When rates rise, some customers benefit and some investors pay. When rates fall, a quite different group of customers and investors might divide the costs and benefits in the other direction. Even though this bargain may be fair on average, it usually would not be fair to all parties at all times.

On balance we believe that setting the allowed rate of return equal to the cost of capital is the policy that best meets the criterion of "fairness."

3. Use of the Market-to-Book Ratio as a Guide for Regulators

Our second approach to developing the reasons that the cost of capital should serve as the basis of the allowed rate of return is indirect: we examine the proposition that regulators' actions should make the ratio of a regulated stock's market value to its book value (slightly more than[19]) one. This prescription is frequently heard, but not always agreed to. It turns out to be simply another way of saying that the allowed rate of return should equal the cost of capital. It is worth approaching the topic from this direction because understanding this proposition's premises yields additional insights into the nature of the cost of capital and the "fairness" of alternative policies. It also shows that failure to follow the prescription may prove very costly in the long run.

Why Choose a Market-to-Book Ratio of One?

The market-to-book ratio expresses the market value of the firm's outstanding common stock to the book value of its equity. If the two are equal, the expected return on the book will equal the expected return on the market value of the company, which in turn will equal the cost of capital for a company of that degree of risk.

The Basic Argument

To demonstrate the point, we first must define the determinants of the market value of a company. We start by defining the concept of the present value of a stream of future cash flows. A present-value calculation discounts future expected returns back to the present. The basic formula is

$$PV = \sum_{y=1}^{Y} \left[\frac{CF_y}{(1 + r)^y} \right], \tag{2.1}$$

which translates as

Present value of a stream of future cash flows	=	Sum, over all future years (running from 1 to Y) in which a cash flow is expected, of	$\left(\dfrac{\text{Cash flow expected in year } y}{\text{Sum of one plus the discount rate raised to the } y\text{th power}} \right)$

By definition, the appropriate discount rate in a present-value calculation is the cost of capital. As discussed earlier, the cost of capital depends on business and financial risk and may change over time, depending on such factors as the state of the economy or the rate of inflation.

The market value of a stock, which we shall call MV, equals the present value of the expected cash flows to stockholders, discounted at the current cost of capital appropriate for the stock's risk. These cash flows equal the expected dividends per share, which in turn are determined by the expected earnings of the firm. In principle the cash flows extend into the indefinite future (i.e., Y is replaced by infinity in [2.1]).[20] Changes in the market value of a firm may arise from changes in either its expected cash flows or its cost of capital.

At this point we make two simplifying assumptions: (1) The firm is in a no-growth steady state, so that forecasted earnings and dividends can be treated as perpetual annuities. This assumption is for convenience only; our conclusions would follow for any growth pattern. (2) Rate base equals net book value.

If investors forecast dividends as a perpetual annuity, then equation (2.1) simplifies to $PV = CF/r$, so that $MV = CF/r$.

The expected earnings, E, of a company subject to rate-of-return regulation equal its allowed rate of return, ROR, times its rate base (which we assume equals net book value, BV), assuming other expenses and total sales are correctly forecasted in setting the rates charged to customers. Symbolically, $E = ROR \times BV$.

If the firm does not grow, all earnings can be paid out to investors. (Reinvested depreciation is sufficient to maintain the value of the rate base.) Then the cash flow received by investors equals earnings, so $CF = ROR \times BV$. The market value of the firm's stock is:

$$MV = \frac{CF}{r} = \frac{(ROR \times BV)}{r}. \tag{2.2}$$

The market-to-book ratio therefore equals the ratio of the allowed rate of return to the cost of capital:

$$\left(\frac{MV}{BV}\right) = \left(\frac{ROR}{r}\right) \tag{2.3}$$

Equation (2.3) of course reflects strong simplifying assumptions. But the qualitative conclusions we draw from it hold in most cases. If regulators allow the firm to expect to earn its cost of capital, market value will equal book value ($ROR = r$ implies $ROR/r = MV/BV = 1$, so that $MV = BV$). Conversely, if we observe $MV = BV$, we conclude that investors expect regulators to allow the firm to earn its cost of capital, at least on average. ($MV = BV$ implies $MV/BV = ROR/r = 1$, so that $ROR = r$.)

Possible Complications

These two conclusions hold under a variety of more general assumptions. Thus the assumed constancy of the rate of return, the rate base, and the cost of capital, and the assumed infinite cash flow horizon, are not important. If more general assumptions in these areas were made, the equations would grow more complicated but the same conclusions would be reached. However, some of the assumptions made do lead to important complications.

First, it is important that the *actual* rate of return investors expect the firm to earn on its rate base must equal its cost of capital, not just that the *allowed* rate of return equal the cost of capital. For example, if investors expect a systematic difference between allowed and realized rates of return (the so-called earnings attrition problem), the allowed rate of return would have to be adjusted to offset the expected difference if regulators desire to bring market value into equality with the firm's rate base.

So far we have equated rate base with net book value. This is essentially true with Original Cost regulation, although complications are often encountered.[21] For example, if only part of a firm's business is regulated, book value exceeds rate base. The firm's stock price may differ from book value per share because book value does not measure economic value for unregulated lines of business. The book value and the market value of an unregulated firm's equity may be very different. Thus a market-to-book ratio greater than one does not necessarily indicate superior profitability.

Even if all the firm's *activities* are regulated, there may be some book assets, such as construction work in progress (CWIP), that do not appear in the rate base.[22] This does not necessarily upset our interpretation of the market-to-book ratio, however. Commissions do allow return on CWIP by giving an allowance for funds used during construction (AFUDC). AFUDC is not immediately charged to consumers but reserved for later inclusion in the rate base. The market-to-book ratio will still equal one, however, as long as both the AFUDC rate and the allowed rate of return equal the cost of capital.[23]

Thus a commission might aim at equality of market and book value because they would then know that investors expected the regulated firm's actual average rate of return to equal its cost of capital (assuming Original Cost or equivalent Fair Value regulation). The market-to-book ratio is an indication of how nearly the market expects regulators to achieve this goal.

Does Undervaluation of Unregulated Stocks Imply Regulated Stocks Should Be Undervalued Too?

A number of stocks, particularly those of companies owning large amounts of natural resources such as petroleum, have sometimes been said to be "undervalued." Several explanations for this alleged widespread undervaluation have been offered in the economics literature, but the debate continues.[24] For regulators, the issue is whether such undervaluation implies that market values should be lower than book values for regulated companies as well. Is it "fair" for regulated stocks to be protected against undervaluation when unregulated stocks are not? A closer look at this argument shows that it should not be carried over to regulated firms.

Possible Reasons for Undervaluation

The explanations for undervaluation offered to date include: (1) inflation-induced errors in investors' evaluation of unregulated earnings, because of failure to recognize the increases in asset values due to inflation; (2) an increase in the effective tax rates on *real* corporate income, because taxable book income overstates real income when inflation "renumbers" the dollars in which earnings are measured; (3) increased riskiness in all stocks relative to other investments, perhaps also because of inflation; and (4) a basic decline in the *average* pre-tax profitability of existing capital in the United States, because of changes such as the run-up of energy prices.

Examples may clarify these explanations. First, inflation makes conventionally reported book earnings very misleading. If the resale or replacement value of an asset increases from $1 million to $1.1 million during a year, the $100,000 difference is not reported as earnings. The first explanation is that investors simply do not recognize how valuable these hidden earnings are and so underprice stocks.

Second, income taxes are applied to book earnings, which rely on historical rather than current costs for capital assets. Straight-line, ten-year book depreciation of a $1-million asset is $100,000. But if the asset would cost $1.5 million new today, "using up" one tenth of its productive life this year represents a cost of $150,000. The extra $50,000 of true cost is not deducted as an expense in computing tax liability, so the company must pay taxes on it. Real tax rates have increased. (Note that the hidden real income from asset appreciation cuts against this argument.)

The third explanation is that stocks, for whatever reason, have proved to be poor inflation hedges, and rational investors consider this in choosing among investments. Money that went into the stock market in the 1960s was invested in houses, gold, stamps, and other nonfinancial assets in the '70s. The result has been a fall in the value of stocks.

The fourth explanation is that the physical assets the stockholders own were designed to use cheaper raw materials, especially energy. When energy prices rose dramatically, net profits using these now-inefficient assets fell, so their value (measured by their stock price) fell also. An example is the 1974 resale value of a 1973 "gas guzzling" car.

Applicability to Public Utilities

The key point for regulatory policy is that none of these explanations implies that undervaluation should be carried over to regulated stocks.

Asset values of regulated companies do not appreciate with inflation, at least under Original Cost or equivalent Fair Value rate bases. All of the inflation compensation investors are to receive comes in the rate of return underlying current earnings. If inflation-induced errors are responsible, such errors would not occur for regulated companies' stocks.

Under cost-based regulation, taxes are treated as an expense to be recovered from ratepayers. Equityholders do not benefit from a reduction in tax rates, because their revenue requirements are lowered by a like amount.[25] Therefore, it would be inconsistent to force them to bear the cost of an increase in effective tax rates, whether caused by inflation or legislation.

Finally, and in a similar vein, rate-of-return regulation is designed to deny utility equityholders the chance for extraordinary capital gains (from factors such as increased productivity or a decrease in the riskiness of all stocks) except during a limited period between regulatory proceedings. Each proceeding resets rates so that the expected rate of return equals the cost of capital. If utility stockholders are denied the chance for extraordinary gains, it would be inconsistent to require them to bear the extraordinary losses that unregulated companies might face from such changes.[26]

Even if one were certain that unregulated stocks were undervalued, there remains one more fundamental objection to allowing regulated stocks to remain undervalued just because unregulated stocks were. Even for unregulated companies, the undervaluation of the *average* assets underlying a stock does not imply an undervaluation of *incremental* assets (new investment). This safeguard does not apply for regulated firms forced to invest when market value is below book value.

Suppose average pre-tax profitability on old assets has declined for an unregulated firm. Managers require (or at least ought to require) that new investments have a positive net present value when the cash flows are discounted at the cost of capital. If this standard is met, the market value of any new assets will equal or exceed their cost. In other words, prudent managers only make a new investment when the implicit market-to-book ratio *for the new investment* is one or higher.

Under conventional regulation, however, the rate of return on both old and new assets is the same. To force the market value of a regulated firm below its book value, regulators must reduce the *average* allowed rate of return below the cost of capital. This in turn would force the firm to make any *new* investments at a substandard rate of return—a burden to which unregulated firms are never subjected. It is this burden that underlies the objection to "dilution" of a regulated firm's stock when new equity is issued when market value is below book value.[27]

Thus although it may seem attractive to force regulated firms' market-to-book ratios to the levels of unregulated firms, this would often require allowed rates of return substantially above or below the cost of capital. If above, regulated firms would receive a windfall on each new investment; if below, they would suffer a capital loss. In either case the basic standard of cost-based regulation would be violated—and for what end? The *reasons* that unregulated firms' market and book values differ do not apply, or should not apply, to regulated firms.

The Implications of a Conscious Decision Not to Equate Market and Book Value

From the preceding discussion, it should be clear that a decision to permit market value to remain lower (or higher) than book value implies that the average expected rate of return will be lower (or higher) than the company's cost of capital.[28] The longer this condition persists, the more serious the consequences.

In recent years market value is most commonly below—often substantially below—book value. Data for three regulated industries are shown in figure 2.4 in ratio form and in figure 2.5 on a logarithmic scale.[29] Several reasons for the persistent shortfalls over the last decade are possible.

Real energy prices increased substantially during the 1970s, creating serious difficulty for people with lower incomes. During the same period inflation and the cost of capital also increased substantially. Holding back the rate of growth of regulated prices would aid those with lower incomes, and one way to do so is to be slow to recognize the full increases in the cost of capital.

Second, compared to unregulated prices, the conventional rate-base approach requires exaggerated changes in regulated prices following a change in the rate of inflation or a large addition to the rate base.[30] Customers naturally object to such dramatic differences from the pattern of other prices.[31]

The cost of capital reached very high levels in recent years; some regulators may not have believed that such high rates of return were truly necessary to bring forth the capital needed for new investments. Alternatively, regulators may have believed that the cost of capital

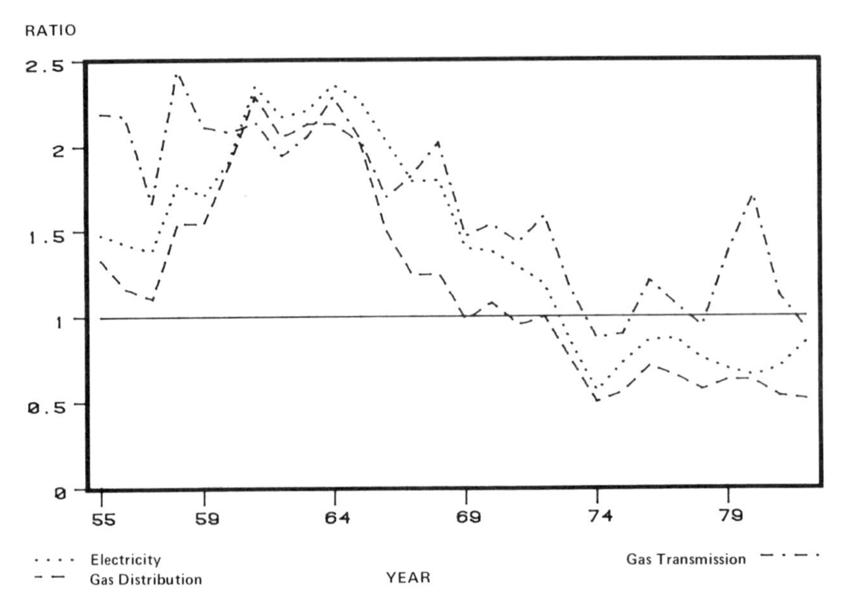

Figure 2.4
Market-to-Book Ratios for Gas and Electric Utilities
Source: Moody's Public Utility Manual.

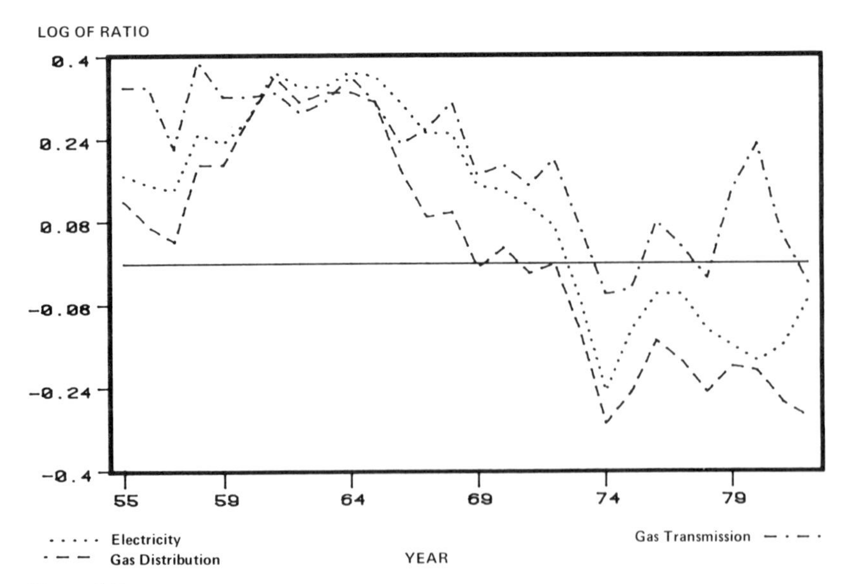

Figure 2.5
Market-to-Book Ratios for Gas and Electric Utilities: Logarithmic Scale

was truly as high as it appeared but may have been responding with a lag in order to smooth the rate of change of regulated prices. (As noted earlier, for this procedure to be "fair" to investors on average, regulators must also respond with a lag when the cost of capital declines; see Kolbe 1983.)

Finally, regulators may have consistently underestimated the cost of capital. In this view, the low market-to-book ratios are a mistake, not the consequence of a deliberate policy.

Regardless of the reasons that regulators might consciously allow market-to-book ratios to remain below one, such a decision implies either that the regulators are substituting their judgment for the market's in deciding how much return is truly required, or that regulators believe the costs of maintaining this policy to be lower than the costs of allowing rates of return high enough to equate market and book values. If the former, regulators must at least recognize that they cannot force the market to share their judgment. If the latter, regulators should recognize that the costs of failing to equate the rate of return with the cost of capital will grow larger the longer the policy persists.[32]

The costs of the policy are the mirror image of the benefits of equating the cost of capital and the rate of return discussed earlier. Given an inadequate rate of return, the value of outstanding stock will fall to where the expected rate return on the lower purchase price equals the cost of capital. Existing shareholders will pay for this fall through a capital loss. If the policy is maintained, new investors are likely to be aware of the chance for such losses to recur, and to require a higher expected rate of return as a result. Also, utility managers can make new investments only by penalizing their existing stockholders, which they will be increasingly unwilling to do as the condition persists. Managers will look for ways to reduce shareholder losses, including deferral of investments and a preference for small investments even if larger investments would be much more efficient.

Utimately, the costs of the policy will be split between the original shareholders and future ratepayers. The short-run benefits will go to current ratepayers.

In our view, the arguments in favor of equating the allowed rate of return with the cost of capital, at least on average, are overwhelming. The remaining chapters assume that this goal is accepted, and turn to the narrower question of how to estimate the cost of capital.

3 The Five Major Methods: Definitions and Conceptual Evaluation

After reviewing testimony and decisions presented in a number of hearings, we concluded that five cost-of-capital estimation methods should be reviewed in detail: Comparable Earnings, Discounted Cash Flow, Capital Asset Pricing Model (CAPM), Risk Positioning, and Market-to-Book Ratio. We chose these methods because they are frequently used, because their use seems likely to become more common, and/or because their use presents unusually subtle problems in application.

1. Evaluative Criteria

Our criteria for evaluating methods of estimating the cost of capital fall into three categories: theoretical (does it work in principle?), practical (how hard is it to use?), and empirical (how well does it seem to work in practice?). Each category has two parts, so there are six criteria in all. The empirical evaluation is contained in the next chapter, to facilitate comparisons among the methods.

The theoretical standards check (1) whether a commission using the method correctly would indeed arrive at a rate of return equal to the cost of capital (logical consistency); and (2) whether a method's assumptions and procedures are consistent with economic theory and an up-to-date understanding of how capital markets work (consistency with theory). The practical criteria examine (1) the availability and objectivity of the required data; and (2) the administrative and similar costs to all parties of a decision to use a particular method. The empirical criteria ask (1) how well the methods seem to work in practice; and (2) the extent to which regulatory commissions have used the methods to set allowed returns.

Logical Consistency and Consistency with Theory

The test for logical consistency checks whether the nature of the method inherently causes the estimated rate of return to miss the cost of capital. The test can be failed in two ways:

1. The method may not be designed to estimate the cost of capital; it may make sense only if regulators aim at a different target. Thus the method may be logically consistent when regulators have other goals.

2. The method may be circular. That is, data needed to apply the method may be affected by investor anticipations of commission actions or even by the very fact that investors know the commission is relying on these data. A commission using such a method will find that the rate of return it sets misestimates the cost of capital because the information it needs is contaminated.

For an example of a method aimed at a different target, suppose a regulatory commission believes that a utility's rate of return should equal the average book rate of return of a group of reference companies in the previous year, which happens to be 12 percent. This 12-percent return will equal the reference companies' cost of capital only by sheer accident, because (among other reasons) any one year's *actual* return is heavily influenced by chance and the business cycle. If these regulators are aiming at the cost of capital, their method is logically inconsistent: it will not hit the target even if they follow every step perfectly (i.e., if they have made the correct calculations in deciding that the reference companies' actual book rate of return was 12 percent last year).

The regulators may instead be trying to enforce a different standard: they may believe it is "fair" for the regulated company to share the actual returns achieved by the reference group of companies, regardless of whether that return equals the cost of capital. Their approach is logically consistent with this different standard but will lead to the problems described in chapter 2: over- and under-payment for capital and over- and under-investment in plant and equipment.

For an example of a circular method, suppose that a commission for a company with a low market-to-book ratio announces that it is going to set a rate of return at the next hearing that will make the market-to-book ratio of the company equal to one. The new allowed rates will go into effect immediately after the hearing. Investors believe that the commission will do as it says, but the commission's plan (not announced) is to raise or lower the allowed rate of return already in effect based on the market-to-book ratio at the time of the hearing. What would happen?

At the time of the hearing, the commission will find that the market-to-book ratio already equals one, because investors have bid up the market price in anticipation of a higher rate of return. Based on this market-to-book ratio, the commission's procedure would indicate that the old rate of return is adequate. If they follow their plan and announce that the new rate of return is equal to the old, investors will be disappointed and the market-to-book ratio will fall to its original level.

The problem is that the commission in the last step used the market-to-book ratio to set the rate of return, but this ratio was determined by investor anticipations of the commission's actions. Such a method of setting the rate of return is circular: the data needed to use it (in this case, market-to-book ratios) are biased by the commission's decision to use the method. The method fails the logical consistency test.

A logically inconsistent method should be either modified to eliminate the inconsistency, applied in the way that minimizes the inconsistency's practical effect, used with extreme caution, or thrown out.

We also ask whether a method's assumptions and procedures are in accord with economic theory and the modern understanding of how capital markets work (the consistency with theory test). This might lead us to ask whether a method's assumptions are realistic. But perfect realism is unattainable, so we end up asking how easily a method's assumptions are violated and how serious the violations are.

These are practical and empirical questions. But there are theoretical issues, as well. Every method for estimating the cost of capital rests on a more general theory of how capital markets work. The method is suspect to the extent that the underlying theory is inconsistent with accepted finance theory or has failed in careful statistical tests. Some people may dismiss recent theoretical developments as information that is of no help in fixing the allowed rate of return in actual practice. This is a mistake. Every method rests on one theory or another; it is important to know if the theory underlying one's preferred method has been discredited or updated.[1]

No method can claim theoretical perfection, much less perfection in practice. The real issue is how robust the method's answers are when the economy deviates from the assumptions underlying the theory. The check for theoretical consistency can be summed up in a series of questions.

Does routine application of the method automatically reflect changes in general factors we know to influence capital costs, such as the rate of inflation, and specific features of particular companies that we know affect the companies' costs of captial, such as their relative risk? How serious are the inevitable differences between theory and practice likely to be for one method relative to the others? Do reasonably easy ways exist to adjust a method's results to reflect the differences between theory and practice?

Data Requirements and the Method's Costs

An ideal method's required data would meet two standards. First, the required information should be directly observable from readily available sources. Stock prices and dividends are observable; betas (the key parameter in the Capital Asset Pricing Model) and anticipated dividend growth rates (needed in the Discounted Cash Flow method) are not. Because many methods rely in part on estimated variables, the relative difficulty of obtaining good estimates is also important. For example, there is more diversity in the ways analysts estimate dividend growth rates than in the ways they estimate beta, reflecting in part what seems to be a greater difficulty in obtaining consistent, conceptually plausible estimates.

Second, the information should be objective and not dependent on widely varying or arbitrary rules. Reported earnings (needed for the Comparable Earnings method) are directly observable but depend on the selection the firm has made among a number of generally accepted accounting rules. These rules may not be arbitrary for the purposes for which they were designed, but their *effects* may be arbitrary when earnings are used for other purposes, such as rate-of-return evidence. Also, the rules themselves may be controversial even in their intended application.

In addition to the difficulty of gathering and processing the data, there may be substantial costs of other kinds. More elaborate methods may require greater expertise and experience to evaluate the available data and cope with the inevitable data problems. Other parties to a proceeding may wish to obtain similar expertise in order to understand fully the initial analysis. As a result, the commission may be faced with a complex body of testimony on which to base a decision.

More elaborate methods may also require additional time to explain and review, delaying the time between filing for a rate increase and approval of final rates. Such delays tend to hurt all parties, including commissions, who lose because the longer (and possibly more frequent) hearings involve a greater workload and perhaps a greater backlog.

Accuracy in Practice and Frequency of Use

It is not possible to test directly the accuracy of the cost-of-capital estimates resulting from the various methods. A direct test for accuracy requires knowing the true cost of equity capital for the firms in the sample. But if we knew a way to find the true cost of equity capital, we could throw the other methods away and simply use the "true" method.

Thus all empirical tests must be indirect. We want to know if the methods' estimates have sensible properties when observed across time and if they pick up important differences among the firms. Some of the specific questions we ask are:

1. Does the estimated cost of equity follow changes in interest rates?[2]

2. How stable are the key parameters? In practice, expert witnesses usually estimate the key parameters of a method from historical data, and use the estimates as a forecast representing investors' current expectations. But how well does one period's experience predict the future?

3. Are each method's estimates robust, that is, insensitive to minor changes in the estimation methods? If not, subjectivity in application is inevitable. Is it necessary to change the estimation method over time in order to get "reasonable" estimates?

4. How different are the predictions of the methods at a given time? Is there an obvious way to identify the sources of disagreement among the methods? Is there a "correction" that could be applied by a commission to a given piece of testimony?

Because we are trying to evaluate the basic reliability of the various methods, we rely on simple procedures uniformly applied to the given sample. In specific testimony a witness might make a number of more sophisticated adjustments to his or her procedures to improve the results. But the *choice* of sophisticated adjustments is subjective, itself a matter for "expert judgment." It seems more useful to evaluate the basic methods using procedures *not* relying on expert judgment.

Although neither acceptance of a method by regulators nor frequency of use is a test of how well the method estimates the cost of capital, both indicate how helpful the various methods have been to regulators. We have reviewed available evidence to determine the acceptability of the various methods to regulators.

A Last Word on the Evaluation

The above six criteria are summarized in Table 3.1. Before we begin the formal evaluations a word of caution is in order. Our discussion aims at making the limitations of each method clear, and states each method's good points quickly. The goal is to highlight the potential

Table 3.1
Summary of criteria applied to cost-of-capital estimation methods

Criterion	Purpose
Theoretical	
Logical consistency	Test whether the method would fail to equate rate of return and cost of capital even if applied perfectly.
Consistency with theory	Examine how easily the method's assumptions can be violated, how serious the violations are likely to be, and if other methods would avoid particular violations.
Practical	
Data requirements	Examine the extent to which the method's required data are directly observable and are objective and not dependent on arbitrary rules.
Related costs	Examine other costs (to all parties) likely to arise from application of the method.
Empirical	
Inferred accuracy	Examine the method's ability to track current capital market conditions, the stability and robustness of its key parameters, and differences in predictions among methods.
Regulatory use	Examine available evidence to see how helpful other commissions seem to have found the method.

problems even for methods whose overall performance is good. But this focus on the bad points should not be misread as condemning all methods.

A better reading is that no single method necessarily gives the "right answer," that all methods must be carefully applied, and that any specific application is most helpful when the probable direction and degree of bias in the method are understood.

2. Comparable Earnings

The Comparable Earnings (CE) method (also known as "comparable industry," "comparable risk," "comparative earnings," and "comparative industry"), traditionally the most widely used and accepted approach, has been challenged increasingly in recent years. There are good reasons for these challenges.

Definition and Example

Analysts using the CE method typically start by selecting a sample of firms believed to be of comparable risk. The procedures used to select the comparable-risk sample vary widely, depending on the expert's judgment of what factors indicate risk and comparability. Financial ratios, capital intensity, the line of business, and many other factors have been used. There seems to be no generally accepted way of defining "comparable risk" for the CE method.

Once the sample is selected, the expert calculates the return on equity, ROE, for companies in the sample. ROE is the *book* rate of return to stockholders: the ratio of book earnings (earnings reported by the company in accordance with generally accepted accounting principles) to the book value of equity. The cost of capital for the regulated company is inferred from the book rates of return for these comparable-risk companies, sometimes as a simple average, and sometimes after additional adjustments.

The CE approach can rest on either of two assumptions (a particular expert does not always make clear which one is intended). The first is that equating the book rates of return of the comparable-risk companies and the regulated company assures that the latter can expect to earn its cost of capital. The other is that "fairness" requires regulated firms to have the same (risk-adjusted) book rates of return as unregulated firms, regardless of whether achieving this goal will equate the regulated firm's rate of return with its cost of capital.

Only the first of these assumptions is consistent with the goal of this book, and so we will give it the most attention. This first assumption can rest on either of two underlying premises: (1) The book rate of return is a good measure of the true rate of return, at least for companies in the comparable-risk sample, and the true rate of return measured over some historical period is equal to the current cost of capital;[3] or (2) The book rate of return is *not* a good measure of the true rate of return but the end result will be satisfactory anyway, because book rates of return for all companies, regulated and unregulated, are subject to the same biases.[4]

The key issue for the CE method is whether its assumptions are sufficiently reasonable to justify its use. Before turning to this issue, however, let us show how the method is applied with a simple numerical example.

In what follows, we assume that the sample of comparable firms has been selected and then show how the ROE for a particular company is computed. Table 3.2 contains selected line items from the financial statements of a hypothetical firm and reports the corresponding *ROE*. The numerator and denominator of *ROE* are found from table 3.2 as follows:

Numerator The book income attributable to common stock is equal to net income less preferred dividends. Net income, which is the "bottom line" of the income statement, equals earnings after interest and taxes. Net income is distributed between preferred stockholders, if any, and common stockholders. In a company with no preferred stock, the entire net income is attributable to common stockholders. If there are one or more classes of preferred stock outstanding, preferred dividends must be subtracted from net income to find the net income attributable to common stockholders.

Denominator The book value of common stock can be calculated in two ways, as "stockholders' equity" less the book value of preferred stock, or as the sum of common stock, paid-in capital, and retained earnings, less treasury stock. In a company with no preferred stock, stockholder's equity is equal to common stockholders' equity. If there are one or more classes of preferred stock outstanding, the book value of preferred stock must be subtracted from stockholders' equity to

Table 3.2
Simplified example: Comparable Earnings method

	1977	1978	1979	1980	1981
Statement of retained earnings[a]					
Net income	$ 98	$ 120	$ 145	$ 147	$ 176
Retained earnings (beginning of year)	293	296	305	334	348
Preferred dividends	26	35	34	38	44
Common dividends	69	76	82	95	113
Retained earnings (end of year)	296	305	334	348	367
Balance sheet (year-end values)					
Preferred stock	333	328	318	364	383
Common stock (par value)	491	540	592	659	745
Paid-in capital	265	286	369	415	460
Retained earnings	296	305	334	348	367
Stockholders' equity	1,385	1,459	1,613	1,786	1,955
Calculation of ROE					
Earnings on common	72	85	111	109	132
Common equity (beginning of year)	—	1,052	1,131	1,295	1,422
Common equity (end of year)	1,052	1,131	1,295	1,422	1,572
Common equity (average)	—	1,092	1,213	1,359	1,497
Return on equity (beginning of year)	—	8.1	9.8	8.4	9.3
Return on equity (average)	—	7.8	9.2	8.0	8.8

[a]This information is often reported in a combined income statement and statement of retained earnings.

obtain common stockholders' equity. *Common stock* is equal to the par value of common shares issued. *Paid-in capital* (sometimes called *Capital surplus* or *Contributed capital in excess of par*) is equal to the excess over par value that was received when the shares were issued. *Retained earnings* is equal to the cumulative net income that has not been distributed as either preferred or common dividends. *Treasury stock* is the book value of common shares that have been reacquired by the company since they were issued. This last item must be *deducted,* not added, to obtain the book value of common stock outstanding.

It is common practice to compute the return on equity as the ratio of net income to the average of the beginning-of-year and end-of-year values of common equity. Sometimes beginning-of-year equity or end-of-year equity alone is used. In principle, the correct approach is to use the beginning-of-year value; however results are likely to be distorted by the addition of external capital (which generates additional income) during the year.

Notice that for a growing firm, the return on equity will be lower if the average equity value is used instead of the beginning-of-year value; it will be lower still if the end-of-year value is used. Furthermore, if either the average or the end-of-year value is used, the ROE does not rise in proportion to net income. The last lines in table 3.1 show the results of using both beginning-of-year and average equity to compute the ROE.

An *ad hoc* procedure could be devised to correct the return on equity for the addition of external capital. One approach would be to multiply the book amounts of new equity by the fraction of the year that they were in service before adding them to the beginning-of-year value. But information on the fraction of the year that new assets were in service may be difficult to obtain, which probably accounts for the practice of using the average of beginning- and end-of-year values.

The cost of *common* equity capital is what poses a problem for the regulator and is the subject of this chapter. The cost of preferred equity (like the cost of debt) can be observed directly in the market, because the promised amount and timing of preferred dividends are fixed. Nevertheless, an analogous book "return on preferred equity" and "return on debt" can be computed. The return on preferred equity is equal to preferred dividends divided by the book value of preferred stock. The return on debt is equal to interest expense divided by the book value of debt. These values are referred to as the "embedded cost" of preferred equity and debt.

Logical Consistency and Consistency with Theory

Whether the Comparable Earnings method is logically consistent depends on the advocate's definition of a "fair" return and on the assumed relationship between the book rate of return and the true rate of return. Two cases, representing two goals that the analyst might be pursuing, need to be distinguished.

Possible Goals

The first possible goal that the analyst might pursue is that used in this book: the allowed rate of return should equal the cost of capital.

Then the CE method is logically consistent only if the analyst is willing to assume both that the equality of book rates of return implies the equality of true rates of return and that these true rates of return are equal to the cost of capital.

These assumptions must in turn rest on one of the underlying premises noted in the discussion of assumptions. That is, the past true rate of return earned by the comparable-risk firms must equal their cost of capital (at least on average), and either the observed book ROEs equal the true rate of return (again at least on average), or the biases between book ROEs and the true rate of return are the same for the comparable-risk firms and the regulated firm in question.

In the second case, the analyst is *not* willing to accept one of these underlying premises. If this is true, that analyst's application of the CE method is logically inconsistent with our goal. Consistency is regained only if a quite different goal is substituted: if "fairness" requires equal book rates of return regardless of what is implied for true rates of return relative to the cost of capital.

If a commission decides it agrees with this alternative concept of "fairness" (despite the costs of such a decision), the CE method is logically consistent with that commission's chosen goal, but not with our goal. In the remainder of this discussion we assume that the commission does *not* agree, and therefore attempts to set the rate of return equal to the cost of capital. (After all, our purpose is to evaluate cost-of-capital estimation methods.)

The logical consistency of the CE method with the goal of this book turns on whether equating book rates of return is likely to allow the regulated firm to expect to earn its cost of capital, the issue addressed under the consistency with theory criterion. If the CE method fails the test of consistency with theory, it therefore also fails the test of logical consistency with this book's goal.[5]

In fact the CE method's consistency with theory is weak. The assumptions underlying it are likely to be violated in any practical case. Moreover, there is no simple way to tell whether the CE results will over- or understate the cost of capital.

One problem is that the sample of comparable-risk firms selected by a witness may earn more or less than the cost of capital over any given period. An even more fundamental problem is that the book rate of return based on generally accepted accounting principles will equal the true rate of return only by accident.[6]

Difference of Earned Returns from the Cost of Capital

The rate of return of a company may exceed or fall short of the cost of capital during any given period. Chance or unforeseen developments can cause *realized* returns for any company over any given period to differ from *expected* returns. The resulting differences can create problems for any estimation method that relies on historical data. Estimation methods try to minimize this problem by using a sample of data large enough so that the chance errors tend to cancel out.

The difference between realizations and expectations makes the results of comparable-earnings analyses especially difficult to interpret. Any sample period during which earnings are measured may be an unusually good or unusually bad period for firms in the comparable-risk sample. If so, realized earnings will exceed or fall short of normal earnings. This suggests that the book rates of return used in a comparable-earnings study should be computed over a long period of time—but just how long is difficult to say. We believe that most of the postwar period would be required to obtain estimates with acceptable precision. By way of illustration, rates of return in the corporate sector were unusually high during the 1960s and unusually low during the 1970s.[7] Thus book returns might yield an upward-biased estimate of the cost of capital during the 1960s and a downward-biased estimate during the 1970s.[8]

Another source of difference between realized and expected returns is that companies, by good luck, good management, or market power, may make investments with an average rate of return in excess of the cost of capital. Companies may also make equivalent "bad" investments, but those making too many bad investments will not survive. In the long run, a sampling problem could be created for book ROEs even if book and true rates of return were the same: the average of the surviving unregulated companies' *realized* true rates of return could be in excess of their costs of capital, since some of the observations on realized returns below the cost of capital would have disappeared with the bankrupt firms.

Methods that rely on security prices have a built-in correction for this problem. When investors become aware of above-normal profitability for a specific company, the price of the company's stock is quickly bid higher, until the expected return on the higher purchase price equals the cost of capital. While original stockholders gain, new stockholders can only expect to earn the company's cost of capital. The stock price at any time reflects current expectations.

No such adjustment mechanism exists for book rates of return. Since book earnings do not distinguish between "excess" and normal returns, the CE method is especially susceptible to this source of difference. The only way to avoid the problem within the CE method is by the exercise of expert judgment, removing companies that investors expected to do abnormally well or poorly from the comparable-risk sample. But the expert may have trouble distinguishing those companies doing especially well or poorly because of chance differences between realizations and expectations (which should be left in the sample) from those whose *expected* return is different from their cost of capital (which should be excluded from the sample).

Basic Problems with Accounting Data

The more serious difficulty for the CE approach is that the accounting rate of return for a company or an industry is a poor estimate of the true rate of return, particularly in an economy characterized by high and variable rates of inflation. No simple adjustment will eliminate this problem.

The source of difficulty is that the accounting concepts of income and value are not the same as the corresponding economic concepts. Accounting numbers derived from generally accepted accounting principles do not measure—nor do they purport to measure—income and value as defined by economic theory. It is not surprising, therefore, that accounting measures of return on investment do not coincide with economic measures.

Much of the confusion regarding the meaning of accounting numbers arises from the fact that the vocabulary of accounting contains many of the same terms as the vocabulary of economics. Accounting concepts are not unrelated to economic concepts, but the distinctions between accounting and economic definitions are crucial. Some of the more important distinctions include:

1. In accounting, asset values are defined in terms of acquisition or historical cost. Changes in asset values subsequent to acquisition are not recognized in accounting, other than by means of the accounting depreciation schedule.[9] In economics, asset values are defined in terms of market values or replacement cost. The distinction between accounting and economic definitions of value have implications for the income statement as well as the balance sheet. For example, depreciation, an income statement item, is based on assets, a balance

sheet item; and the cost of goods sold, an income statement item, is based on the value of inventory, a balance sheet item.

2. In accounting, the depreciation schedule is used to write down systematically the original cost of assets with long but finite useful lives. In other words, it is used to match revenues with expenses. In economics, depreciation is defined as the change in the value of an asset. The choice of depreciation schedules for accounting purposes is to a large degree arbitrary. Even if the estimated useful life of assets is correctly chosen, the depreciation formula applied to those assets may bear little relationship to the actual pattern of economic depreciation. Accounting depreciation charges, therefore, will equal economic depreciation only by accident. Again, both income statement and balance sheet items are affected.

3. Accountants exercise considerable discretion in the application of generally accepted accounting principles. This leads to still another problem: two companies, both of which follow generally accepted accounting principles, can have identical financial performance yet report very different accounting earnings.

These are problems of the most fundamental sort. But the problems with accounting numbers are even more severe when the economy is characterized by rapid inflation.

4. Accounting errors due to inflation vary across asset life. Book measures are likely to understate true returns early in an asset's life and overstate them later. A company that holds mostly old assets will tend to have overstated book profits and a company that holds mostly new assets will tend to have understated book profits. The assets themselves tend to grow progressively more undervalued as inflation proceeds.

5. Current assets as well as fixed assets are affected by inflation. The accounting valuation of inventory is the key issue here. If the first-in, first-out method is used to value inventory, then book earnings will tend to overstate true earnings, because the cost of goods sold does not reflect the current (higher) cost of inventory. If the last-in, first-out method is used, so that the cost of goods sold is in line with the current cost of inventory, then the value of inventory recorded on the books will tend to understate the value of inventory. All inventory valuation methods based on historical cost accounting principles suffer from some kind of inflation distortion.

Table 3.3
Inflation-induced biases in one year's book rate of return

	Book value (historical and current dollars)		True value (current dollars, end of year)	
Net income				
Sales		$100		$105
− Costs:				
Wages and benefits		30		31
Materials:				
Materials used (FIFO)	20		24	
Inventory appreciation	0		(10)	
Net materials cost		20		14
Depreciation:				
Value of assets written off	10		20	
Asset appreciation	0		(40)	
Net depreciation		10		(20)
= Pre-tax income		40		80
− Taxes		20		20
= After-tax income		$ 20		$ 60
Value of equity		$200		$400
Rate of return (net income to equity)		10%		15%

Note: We assume that inflation is the only source of bias, that the firm has no debt, that previous inflation has doubled the value of the firm's beginning-of-year assets as measured in end-of-year dollars, and that no assets have been added during the year. Numbers in parentheses are negative.

There are many other conceptual problems with using accounting numbers to compute the realized rate of return. Many assets, for example, are not recorded on the balance sheet at all. A case in point is the accounting treatment of research and development expenditures, which are expensed rather than capitalized for accounting purposes. But the most serious problems are the historical cost principle and the accounting depreciation schedule.

A numerical example may help to clarify the effects of inflation on the accounting rate of return. Table 3.3 reports the book value and true value of earnings and assets for a hypothetical firm with no debt. The example assumes that inflation is the only source of bias. Even so, the nominal[10] book rate of return underestimates the nominal true rate of return by 50 percent.

As illustrated in table 3.3, with continuous inflation book values misstate true values even for current items like sales and wages. The misstatements are larger for items that are mixes of current and historical dollars, such as the changes in the values of inventories and capital assets. (Although not shown in this example, reported earnings also ignore the gain stockholders receive when an increase in inflation erodes the value of long-term liabilities.) Inflation causes misstatements in *changes* in value, which when misstated affect the calculation of net income (the numerator of the rate of return); inflation also causes misstatements of the value of the assets themselves (the denominator of the rate of return).

As a result inflation may end up either increasing or decreasing the reported book rate of return. In periods of inflation, these problems tend to cause book earnings to exceed true *real* earnings but to fall short of true *nominal* earnings. The numerator of the book rates of return used in the CE method is therefore likely to be too small. (Remember that the fair rate of return on a book-value rate base is the *nominal* cost of capital.) However, the book assets in the denominator are understated also. The result is that even the direction of bias in book rates of return cannot be predicted in advance.[11] This is a serious problem for utility ratemaking applications.

Inflation is not the only problem with book rates of return. Even without inflation the accounting depreciation schedule will match the true year-to-year change in the value of the assets only by accident. *Thus, it is not generally possible to say whether a firm's book rate of return overstates or understates its true rate of return, even in an economy with no inflation at all.*

These biases do *not* cancel out by averaging across the assets within a company or across companies, except by accident. Fisher and McGowan 1983 carefully examine the differences between true and accounting rates of return under simplified assumptions favorable to accounting rates of return (no inflation, steady growth, constant true rate of return).

> Hence, only by accident will accounting rates-of-return be in one-to-one correspondence with economic [i.e., true] rates-of-return. We show . . . that the effects involved cannot be assumed to be small—*indeed, they can be quite large enough to account for the entire inter-firm variation in accounting rates-of-return among the largest firms in the United States*. . . . [T]he effects can be very large; *the belief that they are small enough in practice to make accounting rates useful for analytic purposes rests on nothing but wishful thinking*.[12]

Numerous other studies focus on different aspects of the same problem. Examples include Solomon 1970, Cagan and Lipsey 1978, and Brealey and Myers 1981, chapter 12. Collectively, these studies demonstrate that accounting rates of return are not only wrong as estimates of true rates of return—they can easily be *seriously* and *persistently* wrong.

Differences Between Regulated and Unregulated Returns

The problems with accounting returns are further complicated for ratemaking purposes because the kinds and degrees of bias for unregulated firms are different from those for regulated firms.

Under conventional rate-of-return regulation, the value of the rate base is equal to net original cost; depreciation is equal to the change in this value.[13] As we said earlier, the market value of a firm subject to original cost regulation should be equal to the book value of the rate base on average. In contrast, the market value and the book value of an unregulated firm may be vastly different. Book values of regulated firms have more economic meaning than book values of unregulated firms, because the true values of assets (the denominator of the rate of return) and depreciation (an important source of bias in the numerator of the rate of return) are (or are supposed to be) constrained by regulation to equal their book values.

If regulators in fact maintain market-to-book ratios that equal one on average, then book rates of return should be closer to true (nominal) rates of return. Unfortunately this hurts, not helps, the CE approach. Unregulated firms' accounting rates of return are even less likely to measure the accounting rate of return a *regulated* firm should have. If book returns are biased, the CE method could give the correct answer only if the biases were the *same* for regulated and unregulated firms.

If book rates of return are more meaningful for regulated companies, it might seem natural to try to redeem the CE method by relying on a sample of regulated companies, especially since this may be a good way to select a sample of comparable risk. But this approach creates a different pitfall for the CE method: circularity.

Suppose that one regulatory commission makes a mistake in setting the allowed rate of return for a company under its jurisdiction. If another regulatory commission relies on the book rate of return of this company as evidence of the required rate of return, it will copy the mistake. This process could go on *ad infinitum*. Thus the data used in the comparable-earnings method become contaminated by the very use of the method when the comparable-risk sample consists of companies subject to rate-of-return regulation. In this case, the CE method fails the test of logical consistency in a different way.

A Last Word

Although the use of accounting rates of return in regulation creates severe problems, we do not wish to condemn accounting rates of return entirely. It is possible to make theoretically sound attempts to resolve the accounting problems, by focusing on real rather than nominal returns (trying to back out the effects of inflation), working with replacement cost rather than constant-dollar original cost asset values, and examining a large number of companies over a long period of time.[14] However, making a serious attempt to untangle accounting data to reveal true rates of return is vastly more complicated than what is attempted in usual CE applications. As usually practiced the CE method is subject to the serious problems inherent in accounting data.

Data Requirements and the Method's Costs

The data required for CE as conventionally applied are readily obtainable but dependent on a number of accounting rules and chance circumstances (such as the average age of the comparable firms' assets). These rules and circumstances have arbitrary and unpredictable effects. The readily observable data need extensive, complicated adjustments to try to untangle the arbitrary elements and estimate the true rate of return underlying them.

The CE method has been widely used and accepted by a number of expert witnesses and regulatory commissions. In routine applications there should be minimal difficulty in explaining, understanding, and judging the results. Conventional applications of the CE method get good marks on this criterion. We leave the reader to judge whether ease of presentation of a method likely to yield the wrong answer is truly an advantage.[15]

Unfortunately, explaining attempts to untangle accounting data to estimate true rates of return is likely to prove difficult. Unconventional applications aimed at correcting the biases in the CE method may have high related costs. In fact, development and description of a conceptually sound piece of CE testimony might well be the most difficult and expensive approach to estimating the cost of capital.

3. Discounted Cash Flow

The Discounted Cash Flow (DCF) method was the first widely used alternative to the Comparable Earnings method and remains the most widely used alternative today.

Definition and Example

The DCF approach rests on the formula for computing the present value of a cash flow stream, with some important simplifying assumptions. There are several variations on the DCF theme. One of the most common, the Earnings-Price Ratio (EPR) method, is also evaluated in this section.

Basic DCF Approach

The present-value calculation underlying the DCF approach is the same as discussed in chapter 2; its formula is often written as

$$PV = \sum_{y=1}^{Y} \left[\frac{CF_y}{(1 + r)^y} \right], \tag{3.1}$$

which translates as

Present value of a stream of future cash flows	=	Sum, over all future years (running from 1 to Y) in which a cash flow is expected, of	$\left(\dfrac{\text{Cash flow expected in year } y}{\text{Sum of one plus the discount rate raised to the } y\text{th power.}} \right)$

The DCF model relies on the equivalence of the market price of a stock, P, with the present value of the cash flows investors expect from a stock, providing the discount rate equals the cost of capital. It also makes several simplifying assumptions: investors expect the cost of capital (r, the discount rate) to remain constant in the future; the cash flows relevant for the calculation are the dividends, D_y, that stockholders receive in year y;[16] the dividends are expected to grow at a constant rate, g, into the indefinite future (Y in [3.1] is infinite).

Under these conditions, equation (3.1) can be simplified to

$$P_0 = \frac{D_1}{(r-g)}, \tag{3.2}$$

which says that the price of a stock at the time it is purchased (time 0) equals the dividends expected at the end of the first year of ownership, D_1, divided by the cost of capital minus the steady future growth rate of dividends, $(r-g)$.

The DCF approach solves equation (3.2) for the cost of capital, r, to obtain the familiar form:

$$r = \frac{D_1}{P_0} + g \tag{3.3}$$

which says that the cost of capital is the sum of the expected dividend yield at the time of purchase, D/P, and the (steady) expected growth rate of dividends in the future, g.

To understand the DCF method, it helps to remember that (3.2) is the basic equation, which determines P, and that (3.3) is a rearrangement, to estimate r. For example, some economic factors that increase g (such as a higher rate of inflation) will also increase r, and so leave P unchanged. Equation (3.3) is a natural way to think of such changes. Other forces that increase g (making especially valuable investments) need not increase r. In such cases P will also rise, and a focus on (3.3) could obscure the fact that r is unchanged even though g has changed.

To make use of (3.3) to estimate the cost of capital, one needs the current stock price, an estimate of expected dividends over the next year, and the estimated long-term growth rate of dividends. Dividends and the expected growth rate can be estimated in several ways.

If the DCF model is being applied prospectively, next year's dividends are often estimated by multiplying this year's dividends by the estimated rate of growth. If the model is being applied retrospectively to estimate the cost of capital in some historical period, the actual dividends during that historical period can be used, on the assumption that investors expected the dividends that actually were paid.

However, the selection of the expected growth rate, g, is more difficult and subject to debate. Several approaches are common.

1. Use the historical growth rate of dividends over some period, often five or ten years. Sometimes past growth in earnings or book value per share is used as a proxy for dividend growth, because dividends are changed by firms in discrete jumps, so that their estimated growth rate can change noticeably with the exact starting and ending points of the data series.
2. Use forecasts of growth rates published by investment services, since investor expectations are the desired quantity.
3. Use the "sustainable growth" rate, measured as the rate of return on book equity, *ROE*, times the proportion of earnings that is retained within the firm, b, instead of being paid out as dividends. That is, the ratio of dividends to earnings is $(1-b)$.

The bases of the first two approaches should be clear, but the basis of the third may be less so. The third approach recognizes that if the firm is earning exactly its cost of capital, future growth in dividends for existing equity can only come if part of the overall return to investors is plowed back instead of being paid out. Both historical and forecast values of *ROE* and b are used to estimate g. Forecast values are thought to adjust more readily for recent changes (such as an increase in expected *ROE* because of an increase in the expected rate of inflation) than historical values of either *ROE* or the actual growth rate of dividends. The retention ratio, b, is usually assumed stable. (Firms' target retention ratios are usually, although not always, stable.)

Sometimes more complicated versions of the DCF formula are used. Some may adjust for the timing of next year's dividend payment. Others may consider the issuance of new stock. While such changes may add some precision, we think they should not be allowed to distract from the more fundamental concerns with the DCF approach. As with other methods, witnesses using a variation of the basic approach must explain the reasons that their formula differs from the basic formula, why they think their formula is better, and how much difference it makes to use their formula instead of the usual formula.

Earnings-Price Ratio Approach

An important variant of the DCF method is the Earnings-Price Ratio (EPR) approach. It also can be derived as a special case of a general valuation formula. Because it requires more stringent assumptions it is less widely used than DCF as a stand-alone method.

The basic EPR formula is[17]

$$r = \frac{E}{P}, \tag{3.4}$$

which says that the cost of capital equals the ratio of book earnings to the market price of the stock.

As we said, the EPR is a variation of the DCF model. If the growth rate equals the ratio of retained earnings to the market price of the stock, equations (3.4) (EPR) and (3.3) (DCF) are equivalent. This can be seen by the following manipulation of equation (3.4):

$$\begin{aligned} r &= \frac{E}{P} \\ &= \frac{(D+RE)}{P} \\ &= \frac{D}{P} + \frac{RE}{P} \\ &= \frac{D}{P} + g, \text{ if } g = \frac{RE}{P}, \end{aligned}$$

where RE is retained earnings.[18]

The EPR approach can also be derived as a special case of the following general formula:[19]

$$P = \frac{E}{r} + PVGO, \tag{3.5}$$

which says stock price, P, is equal to the present value of current earnings, E, if they never grow,[20] plus the present value of growth opportunities ($PVGO$). $PVGO$ reflects investments the firm might make in the future that would increase its value. The EPR approach works if and only if the present value of growth opportunities is zero (PVGO = 0).

However, the present value of growth opportunities is zero only in special cases. If the firm does not grow, so that forecasted future earnings are constant for the indefinite future ($g = 0$), then $PVGO$ equals zero. Alternatively, suppose the firm is growing but only earning the cost of capital ($E = rP$), and that all investments open to it would also earn exactly the cost of capital. Then $PVGO$ equals zero and the EPR approach works. Why? Because *net* present value is the value of earnings over and above the cost of the investment. If the investments earn exactly the cost of capital, their net present value is zero. That is, they are worth only what they cost.

Now suppose the firm is earning more than the cost of capital. Then its growth opportunities add to its stock's present value. *PVGO* must be greater than zero, *P* is higher than justified by today's *E* alone, and *E/P* underestimates *r*. Alternatively, suppose the firm is earning less than the cost of capital. Investors cannot expect this to go on forever; the firm's earnings must recover or eventually it must go out of business.[21] The stock price would be higher than justified by *E*, reflecting investor expectations about when recovery was likely, and *E/P* would again underestimate *r* even if no immediate growth is expected.[22] Finally, suppose investors expect future earnings to decline, perhaps because a period of above-normal profitability is ending. *P* is lower than justified by today's earnings, and *E/P* overestimates *r*.

The chief advantage of the EPR is that it is easy to compute. The chief difficulties are (1) it works only when the actual rate of today's earnings exactly matches the firm's cost of capital *and* the firm has no opportunities to invest at rates of return above the cost of capital; (2) it relies heavily on book earnings, which are poor measures of true earnings, especially in inflationary times; and (3) although it can be viewed as a variant of the DCF approach, its assumptions are stronger and hence more likely to be violated. Unless used only as a very rough check, the EPR is inferior to the DCF approach and the latter should be preferred. For this reason, we will focus only on the DCF formula for the remainder of this section.

Example

The DCF model estimates the cost of equity capital as the sum of two components: the dividend yield and the expected growth rate. The dividend yield is well defined: it equals the ratio of the dividend rate (dividends per share expressed on an annualized basis) to the current price. The expected growth rate, on the other hand, may be estimated in a variety of ways. Table 3.4 shows the calculation of year-end dividend yields for a hypothetical firm. It also reports the raw data necessary to compute the growth rate by methods we will discuss in chapter 4. The steps in the calculation are as follows.

The end-of-year dividend yield is equal to the end-of-year dividend

Table 3.4
Simplified example: Discounted Cash Flow (DCF) method

Dividend yield

Year	Closing price	Dividends per share I	II	III	IV	Yield %
1977	$14 2/8	$0.20	$0.20	$0.20	$0.20	5.6
1978	7 2/8	0.20	0.20	0.20	0.20	11.0
1979	15 4/8	0.20	0.20	0.25	0.25	6.5
1980	19 4/8	0.25	0.25	0.35	0.35	7.2
1981	33 1/8	0.35	0.35	0.45	0.45	5.4

Growth rate

Year	Earnings per share	Dividends per share	Payout rate	Return on equity %
1972	$1.29	$0.45	$0.35	25.0
1973	1.47	0.60	0.41	24.5
1974	1.65	0.60	0.36	24.3
1975	1.34	0.60	0.45	15.4
1976	1.54	0.70	0.45	16.4
1977	1.92	0.80	0.42	18.9
1978	2.19	0.80	0.37	19.4
1979	2.54	0.90	0.35	20.0
1980	2.93	1.20	0.41	20.5
1981	3.50	1.20	0.34	21.9

rate divided by the closing stock price. For the table 3.4 example, in 1981 this value was

$$(4 \times \$0.45)/(\$33\ 1/8) = 5.4\%.$$

If we want to use the trend in earnings per share as the estimated growth rate, we can compute it from the following linear regression model:[23]

$$\log(EPS) = a + gt$$

where $\log(EPS)$ is the natural logarithm of earnings per share, t is the time variable (e.g., 1972, 1973, . . . , 1981), and g is the regression slope coefficient, which is the estimated growth rate. The five-year trend in earnings per share is estimated by using only the five most recent years of data; the ten-year trend is obtained by using the ten most recent years of data. In the particular example reported in table 3.4, the five-year trend in 1981 is equal to 15 percent per year; the ten-year trend in 1981 is equal to 11 percent.

Alternatively, we might look to the sustainable growth rate, which is equal to the product of the retention rate and the return on equity. The retention rate is equal to one minus the dividend payout rate which, in turn, is equal to the ratio of dividends to net income (earnings). In chapter 4, we use the five-year average sustainable growth rate as an estimate of the DCF growth rate. For 1981, this value is equal to 8.1 percent in table 3.4.

The DCF estimate of the cost of equity is given by the following equation:

$$r = \left(\frac{D_1}{P_0}\right) + g = \left(\frac{D_0}{P_0}\right)(1 + g) + g.$$

The model calls for the *next period* dividend yield, but we observe the current dividend yield. We estimate next period's value by multiplying the current dividend yield by one plus the expected growth rate. Suppose we wish to use the ten-year trend in earnings per share for the expected growth rate. Then the DCF cost of equity at the end of 1981 is equal to

$$r = (0.054)(1 + 0.11) + 0.11 = 0.170 = 17\%.$$

It is important to note that different ways of estimating g can give quite different values. For example, the five-year EPS trend (15 percent) leads to $r = 21.2$ percent, while the five-year average sustainable growth rate (8.1 percent) leads to $r = 13.9$ percent. Some of the reasons for this variation will be made clear by our later discussion.

Logical Consistency and Consistency with Theory

The DCF method does attempt to measure the cost of capital and so is logically consistent with the standard we recommend. However, a strictly mechanical application of the method could create problems in achieving this goal if the forecast of the growth rate, g, were to depend in large part on past decisions of the commission regarding this utility. While possible in principle, this problem would not be serious in practice, at least not for long.

This one potential logical consistency problem may be seen most clearly when g is estimated by a forecast of the rate of return on book equity, *ROE*, times the retention ratio, *b*, *for the firm being regulated.* Expected *ROE* is precisely what the commission sets in selecting an allowed rate of return on book equity. If a too-high forecast of the *ROE* that investors expect resulted in a too-high *g*, a commission relying on the estimate would also set the rate of return too high, thereby partially fulfilling the too-high prophecy of *ROE*. If at the next hearing the commission relied on this new *ROE*, it could aim even higher, and so on.

The problem is unlikely to be serious because the DCF method also relies on the market price of the stock, which would signal investors' surprise at the unexpectedly high allowed rate of return by jumping in value. Such a jump should lead to a lower dividend rate (the first part of the DCF formula) and a more cautious application of *ROE* forecasts at the next hearing. Thus the method tends to be self-correcting. Moreover, the entire problem is avoided if the DCF method is applied to a broad sample of firms in the same industry, instead of only to forecasts of values for the firm being regulated.

Note that a jump in stock price is *not* proof that the allowed rate of return exceeds the cost of capital. It only indicates that the allowed rate of return exceeds what investors expected before the results of the hearing were announced. If the jump took the ratio of market-to-book value over one, the regulators should suspect that the new allowed rate of return exceeds the cost of capital. If the jump leaves the market-to-book ratio below one, the commission should suspect that the allowed rate of return is still below the cost of capital.

Although the DCF approach almost always passes the logical consistency test, consistency with theory presents more problems. Like the Comparable Earnings method, the DCF method relies on strong assumptions that are likely to be violated in practice. However, the consequences of these violations will often be less serious than with CE, because the reasons for the violation in a particular case may provide clues as to whether the DCF results over- or understate the cost of capital.

The DCF approach assumes the company grows on a steady path, with a constant payout ratio and rate of growth of dividends. If this were true, using market value to assess the required rate of return would assure that investors' perceptions of the company's risks were considered, and the DCF estimate would be a reliable estimate of the cost of capital. Consistency with theory would be achieved—and achieved far more easily than with the CE approach. The important issue is what happens to the DCF approach when this assumption is not true.

Potential Problems

The effect of a violated assumption on the DCF approach depends on the reason for the violation. For example, the assumption that investors expect steady growth forever need not be crucial. The approach can accommodate fluctuations in profitability, payout, and dividend growth, as long as *forecasted* dividends and stock prices exhibit a stable growth trend. In other words, "noise" in growth rates is acceptable if the trend is maintained—although "noise" does make it harder to discern the underlying trend.

It is difficult to apply the DCF approach when a company is in transition between growth paths. This is important in practice because the company's nominal cost of capital (the cost of capital including compensation for anticipated inflation) tends to change every time the rate of inflation changes. Growth trends may change also. Thus periods of variable rates of inflation will tend to produce historical data that do not fit within the DCF assumptions, even if the business and financial risks of the company remain constant.[24]

An Example

An example may help convey potential problems. Suppose a company is on a steady path, with a dividend yield of 8 percent and a growth rate of 4 percent. The DCF cost-of-capital estimate is 12 percent, which we assume equals the firm's cost of capital and is the rate allowed by regulators at the outset. What happens if the rate of inflation suddenly goes from 7 to 10 percent? How is the DCF calculation affected? Several cases should be distinguished.

Let us assume that there is no regulatory lag, so that investors expect (and regulators grant) an immediate increase in the allowed rate of return to 15 percent when inflation accelerates. Since the increased rate of return is received immediately, stock price remains at book value, despite the three-percentage-point increase in the inflation rate and the nominal cost of capital.

If the extra income is all paid out, the dividend yield increases by three percentage points to 11 percent, but the growth rate remains at 4 percent. (Since the stock price is unaffected, any increase in the cash dividend raises the dividend yield proportionately.) In this case a DCF estimate based on the historical growth gives the right answer, because investors expect growth to continue at 4 percent.

If the extra income is plowed back, expected future growth would increase from 4 to 7 percent. A DCF estimate based on historical growth rates would understate the true cost of capital. Note also that DCF applications assuming a constant retention ratio, b, in effect assume that the company would increase the growth rate by $(3 \times b)$ percent, and increase the dividend yield by $[3 \times (1 - b)]$ percent. The sustainable growth approach gives the right answer if the *new* retention ratio is used, but estimates based on past average retention ratios could easily be wrong.

Thus even if all investors agree on what has happened to inflation, how inflation affects the cost of capital, and that regulators will respond promptly to the new conditions, the DCF components can change. If dividends and expected growth rates are estimated from historical data, including historical retention ratios, changes in the cost of capital may not be reflected in DCF estimates.

The addition of regulatory lag to the example complicates matters even more. Investors know that the allowed rate of return will remain below the new cost of capital at least until the next hearing and perhaps longer (if the evidence presented in the next hearing fails to persuade the commission that a 3-percent increase in the allowed rate of return is justified). How are the components of the DCF calculation affected in this case?

The market value of the stock will fall, so that the actual dollar returns that investors expect to realize on the new, lower price will yield the new 15-percent cost of capital. The longer the expected regulatory lag, the more the price of the stock will fall. The dividend yield will increase, and will increase more if regulatory lag is longer. Also, future dividends are unlikely to grow at a steady rate. The assumptions underlying the DCF calculation may thus be violated (the violations may not be serious if the regulatory lag is short).

Ironically, if regulatory lag exists at all, the only case in which the DCF assumptions are exactly right occurs when regulatory lag is infinite. If the regulators *never* respond to increased inflation, then historical growth rates may be an excellent forecast of future growth. If investors use this forecast, the market price falls, the dividend yield increases accordingly, and the DCF calculation using the new, higher dividend yield and the old growth rate correctly estimates the cost of capital. This works only as long as commissions fail to raise the rate of return toward the cost of capital. As soon as commissions begin to act on the new DCF estimates to increase allowed rates of return, the market price climbs, the historical DCF growth rate again underestimates what investors expect, and the DCF calculation again falls short.

When regulatory lag is not infinite, the problems discussed initially still exist after the commission acts: the company may respond by increasing dividends, the growth rate, or some combination of the two. Historical data may not be a reliable guide.[25]

Evaluation of Possible Solutions

One apparent solution to such problems is to use more recent growth rates. This brings its own problems, however. Over short periods chance or changes in general business conditions cause unexpected fluctuations in earnings and growth. Data taken from longer periods are less likely to be biased by differences between actual and expected performance but more likely to miss changes in expectations.

In practice, five- and ten-year growth rates seem to be used most often. Unfortunately, changes in expectations—especially expected inflation—are quite likely in periods much shorter than five years. At the same time, even ten years is not long enough to assure the absence of significant differences between realizations and expectations (see chapter 4 for examples of DCF applications using both five- and ten-year estimates). There are no easy answers to the problems created by a transition in growth paths.

However, if the problems with a DCF calculation result from broad forces such as a change in inflation (as opposed to company-specific factors such as diversification or acquisitions that change the risk-and-return pattern of the stock), there are clues to the direction of the bias in the DCF estimate. If inflation is now higher than the average during the historical period used to estimate g, chances are that a DCF estimate relying on the historical g is too low.

Making use of this information can still be difficult. It probably would not be appropriate to simply add the difference between historical and current inflation to the DCF estimate, because the market price may have changed in response to expected regulatory lag. The "right" correction to the DCF estimate will tend to be positive, but less than the percentage increase in the rate of inflation. The same comments apply in the other direction if today's expected inflation has decreased below the average during the historical period supplying the data.

If the risk of the company changes for firm-specific reasons, the DCF method has even greater difficulty. Because the method attempts to estimate the required rate of return directly (rather than first estimating risk and then the current return required for that degree of risk), there is no easy way to adjust the DCF results for a change in risk.

For example, the required rate of return on the stock of an electric utility that acquired a new line of business (say, a chain of department stores) would reflect both electric-utility business risk and department-store business risk. The cost of capital depends on the risk of the particular investment, so the allowed rate of return on the utility rate base should reflect the risk and cost of capital of the electric-utility line of business not that of running department stores. The diversified utility's future patterns of dividends and growth will be different from those on which the utility's DCF estimates were traditionally based. The commission has somehow to untangle the combined effects of the two lines of business to find the required rate of return for the electric utility assets; the DCF approach, which does not control for either changes in risk or differences in risk in different lines of business, offers little help in such cases. If many utilities diversify, even looking at DCF estimates for other companies in the industry may become less helpful than previously.

On balance, the DCF method's consistency with theory is good when the assumption of stability is met, but the method is difficult to apply when market conditions are volatile or the risk of the company changes.

Data Requirements and the Method's Costs

Stock prices, dividend yields, and other ingredients for DCF estimates are easily obtainable, but the true values required (*expected* dividends and *expected* growth rates) are unobservable. And in periods when investors are not likely to expect steady growth, interpretation of the historical data will require expert judgment. The DCF method gets good marks on this criterion in stable times but poor marks in unstable times.

The DCF method is second only to the Comparable Earnings approach in its history of use and acceptability. A large body of testimony and decisions use or consider the method. Many regulators and their advisors have the experience necessary to understand its strengths, weaknesses, and correct application. The DCF method gets good marks on this criterion.

4. Capital Asset Pricing Model

The Capital Asset Pricing Model (CAPM) is a relatively new way to estimate the cost of capital in regulatory hearings, although its use appears to be growing. It is a conceptual model of capital market equilibrium that has been widely used in finance and economics since the mid-1960s. Because it is a relative newcomer to regulatory proceedings and because its approach is fundamentally different from the Comparable Earnings and DCF methods, we will explain in detail how and why the method is supposed to work.

Definition and Example

CAPM refers to both a theory and a method used in rate hearings. Much of the discussion in finance theory considers the kinds of risks for which investors demand compensation, how to measure those risks, and how to calculate the rate of return the market is currently offering to investors for bearing a particular degree of risk. The CAPM of Sharpe 1964, Lintner 1965, and others was the first equilibrium model of risk and return in capital markets.[26] It uses the Markowitz 1952 treatment of the portfolio-selection problem as a framework for analysis.

In the Markowitz analysis of the portfolio-selection problem, investors choose among securities on the basis of the mean (expected value) and variance (risk) of the rate of return. Markowitz concluded that investors would hold "efficient" portfolios—portfolios with the highest expected return for a given variance or the lowest variance for a given expected return. Sharpe, Lintner, and others use these propositions to develop a model of risk and return in capital markets.

We must emphasize that portfolio theory and the capital asset pricing model are not the same. Portfolio theory is widely accepted as a framework for the analysis of capital markets; the CAPM is based on a specific set of assumptions about how capital markets work. The concept of portfolio risk makes sense even if one does not believe that the CAPM itself is correct.

Portfolio Theory as a Framework for Analysis

Common sense suggests that the risk associated with any investment is that the rate of return on that investment will turn out to be less than expected. That risk is a function of the variability of future returns. Intuitively, the range of possible rates of return on a risky investment will be greater than for safer investments. However, a key issue in finance is identification of the kinds of risk and variability that are important to investors.[27]

A natural first definition for risk is a measure of the total variability of possible returns, such as the variance or the standard deviation of the rate of return about its mean.[28] A large standard deviation would indicate high risk. But this definition turns out to be inadequate.

Most securities are held in fairly well diversified portfolios. The risk of a security in the context of a portfolio is different from the risk of a security viewed in isolation. It is the contribution a security makes to the risk of a portfolio that is relevant. The distinction is crucial because much of the volatility of a security is uncorrelated with the volatility of other securities.

The standard deviation of returns on a portfolio depends on the standard deviations of the returns on the securities included in the portfolio and on the correlation among these returns. As long as security returns are less than perfectly correlated (as long as chance occurrences can affect the returns on some investments without making the returns on all investments move in the same direction at the same time), the portfolio's risk will be less than the average riskiness of the investments it contains. The rates of return on some investments tend to be high while others tend to be low; this reduces average variability—the "swings" cancel one another out.

Thus diversification causes the standard deviation of a portfolio to be less than the average standard deviation of the stocks that make up the portfolio. As additional investments are added to a portfolio, its standard deviation declines toward a minimum determined by the degree of correlation among the investments in the portfolio. The result is that the portfolio may be less volatile than even the most stable asset contained in it.

This idea is illustrated in figure 3.1. The rate of return on each stock is assumed to have a standard deviation of 30 percent per year; different lines in figure 3.1 show different degrees of correlation among the stocks' returns. The lower the correlation among the returns, the faster and farther the portfolio's standard deviation declines.

As illustrated in figure 3.2, the standard deviation of a portfolio's

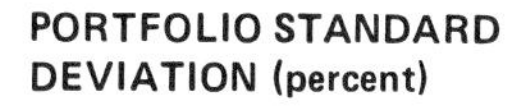

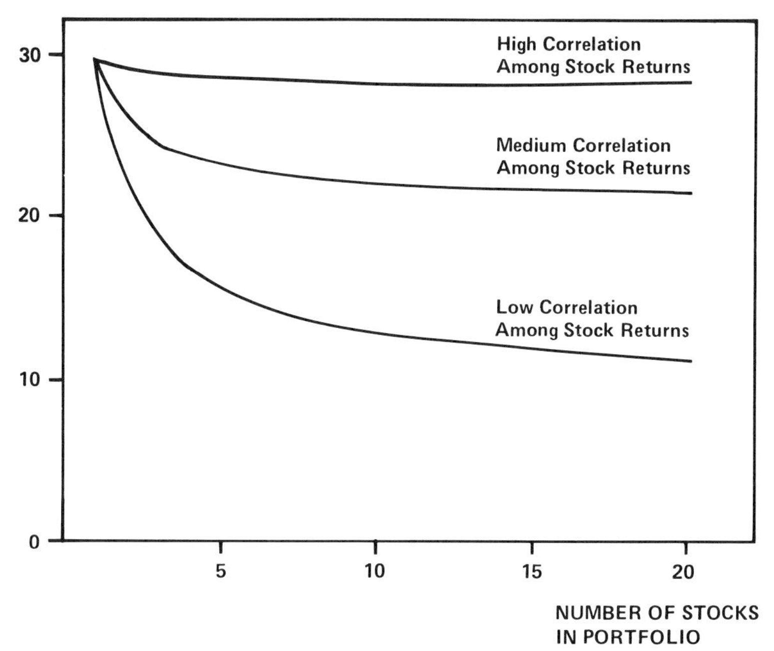

Figure 3.1
Effects of Diversification on the Standard Deviation of a Portfolio

returns can be divided into two components: (1) diversifiable risk (sometimes called "unsystematic" or "unique" risk), which declines to zero as the number of securities in the portfolio becomes large; and (2) nondiversifiable risk ("systematic" or "market" risk), which cannot be eliminated by adding securities to the portfolio.

The risk an asset adds to a portfolio is its contribution to the second component, the nondiversifiable risk of the portfolio. This contribution in turn depends on two factors: the extent to which the asset tends to move in the same direction as the rest of the portfolio, and the extent to which those moves are large or small relative to the moves of the rest of the portfolio.

For example, the price of gold is hard to predict and historically has been very volatile. An investor who put all of his or her assets in gold would be exposed to the possibility of large losses. Nevertheless, gold may properly be considered a conservative investment for the diversified investor, because movements in gold prices tend to be independent of movements in other asset values. Thus a moderate investment in gold stabilizes the value of the total portfolio.

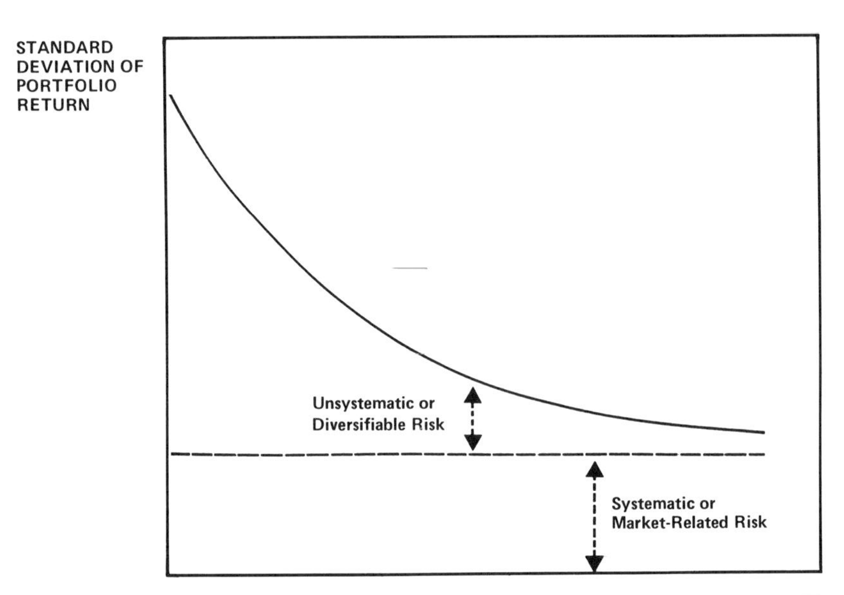

Figure 3.2
Systematic and Unsystematic Risk

The Beta Measure of Risk
In the CAPM, the key risk measure is known as *beta*. An asset's beta combines the volatility of the asset's returns and the correlation of those returns with other assets into a single measure.

The first factor in beta is the width of the average swing in the asset's value relative to the average swing in the portfolio's value. This can be measured by the standard deviation of the asset's returns divided by the standard deviation of the portfolio's returns.

The second factor in beta is the correlation between the asset's moves and the portfolio's moves. A correlation of 1 implies the asset's returns *always* move up when the portfolio's returns move up. A correlation of −1 implies the asset's returns always move *down* when the portfolio's return moves *up*. A correlation of 0 implies the asset and the portfolio move independently of each other.

The product of the correlation and the ratio of the standard deviations is the asset's beta *with respect to that portfolio*.[29]

An important conclusion of the CAPM is that all investors hold the "market portfolio," a portfolio consisting of shares of all stocks. One way to understand this conclusion is to note that such a portfolio would provide maximum diversification. Investors would calculate each asset's beta with respect to "the market." Few investors literally hold the market.[30] However, the returns of well-diversified portfolios are highly correlated with market movements. Thus asset betas measured relative to the market are attractive general measures of asset risk. Betas measured with respect to the market are also the sole measure of asset risk in the CAPM.

The Mathematical Definition of Beta

The usual way to define beta starts from the "covariance" of the asset and the portfolio, here taken to be the market. If r_j is the rate of return on asset j and r_m is the rate of return on the market, the covariance of the two, $\text{cov}(r_j, r_m)$, is defined by

$$\text{cov}(r_j, r_m) \equiv E[(r_j - \bar{r}_j)(r_m - \bar{r}_m)] \equiv \sigma_{jm}, \tag{3.6}$$

which says the covariance is defined as the expected value of the product of the difference between a randomly drawn value of r_j and its mean and a randomly drawn value of r_m and its mean.

As noted earlier, the variance of a random variable, in this case r_m, is defined as

$$\text{var}(r_m) \equiv E[(r_m - \bar{r}_m)^2] \equiv \sigma_m^{\ 2} \tag{3.7}$$

where σ_m is the standard deviation of the rate of return on the market, r_m.

The beta of asset j with respect to the market is defined as

$$\beta_j \equiv \frac{\sigma_{jm}}{\sigma_m^{\ 2}}, \tag{3.8}$$

which says that beta is defined as the ratio of the covariance of r_j and r_m to the variance of r_m. If ρ_{jm} is defined as the correlation between r_j and r_m, the covariance of r_j and r_m can be written as

$$\sigma_{jm} = \rho_{jm}\,\sigma_j\sigma_m. \tag{3.9}$$

Together, equations (3.7) through (3.9) imply the explanation of beta given above, which algebraically is

$$\beta_j = \rho_{jm}\frac{\sigma_j\sigma_m}{\sigma_m^{\ 2}} = \rho_{jm}\left(\frac{\sigma_j}{\sigma_m}\right). \tag{3.10}$$

Thus an asset's beta depends on the correlation of its rate of return with the market's rate of return and on the size of its standard deviation (its variability) relative to the market's.

The CAPM Theory
Portfolio analysis is at the core of the beta concept of risk. The CAPM is a particular theory of market equilibrium (the concept introduced with figure 2.1) that is based on portfolio analysis. The CAPM is widely used to estimate the cost of capital in practical applications in finance (for example, to find the discount rate used to calculate the net present value of a proposed investment). However, the Sharpe-Lintner CAPM and indeed all mean-variance theories of capital market equilibrium remain controversial.

The CAPM theory says first that the beta of an asset with respect to the market portfolio is a complete and sufficient measure of the risk that requires compensation in the market. If one knows the asset's beta, one knows everything necessary about the relative risk of the asset.

An asset that on average fluctuates exactly in step with the market (whose rate of return increases on average by 1 percent when the market's return increases 1 percent) will have a beta equal to one and will be exactly as risky as the market. The returns on a high-beta asset will *amplify* fluctuations in market returns. The wider fluctuations imply more risk: a stock with a beta equal to two will decrease on average by 2 percent when the market decreases by 1 percent. Assets with betas below one fluctuate less than the market and have less risk.

The other step in the CAPM theory is quantifying the amount of compensation required for a given degree of risk, that is, for a given beta. In terms of figure 2.1, the CAPM says that the asset's beta locates the asset's position on the horizontal axis; the second step is to locate the current risk-return line to discover what this risk implies for the asset's required rate of return on the vertical axis.

The CAPM theory says that the current risk-return line is given by

$$E(r_j) = r_f + \{\beta_j \times [E(r_m) - r_f]\}, \quad (3.11)$$

which translates as

$$\begin{array}{l}\text{Expected rate} \\ \text{of return for} \\ \text{asset } j\end{array} = \begin{array}{l}\text{Current risk-} \\ \text{free rate of} \\ \text{return}\end{array}$$

$$+ \left[\begin{array}{l}\text{Asset's} \\ \text{beta}\end{array} \times \left(\begin{array}{l}\text{Expected rate} \\ \text{of return for} \\ \text{the market}\end{array} - \begin{array}{l}\text{Current risk-} \\ \text{free rate of} \\ \text{return}\end{array}\right)\right]$$

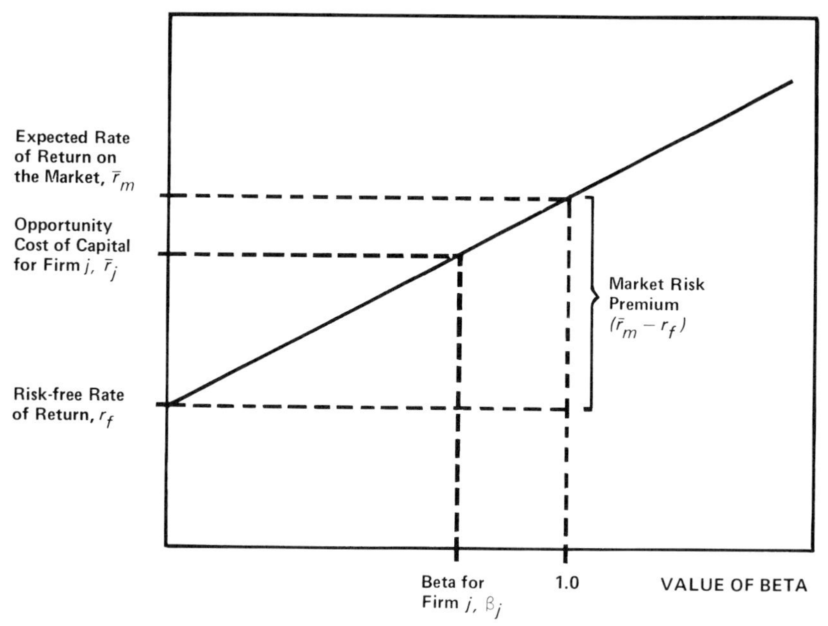

Figure 3.3
The Capital Asset Pricing Model

This is illustrated in figure 3.3. Figure 3.3 specifies both the measure of risk (beta) and the determinant of the slope of the market line ($[E(r_m) - r_f]$), which were both left vague in figure 2.1. The identification of these two specific factors is the distinguishing feature of the CAPM theory. The CAPM theory is far from proved in empirical tests but cannot yet be ruled out.

Use of the CAPM in Rate Hearings

Three values are needed to transform the CAPM theory into a method that can be used in rate-of-return testimony: the firm's beta, the current risk-free rate of return, and the difference between the expected rate of return on the market and the risk-free rate of return. (This difference is called the "market-risk premium.")

The empirical procedures used to estimate these three components of the CAPM formula (equation (3.11)) are generally as follows:

β. Applications of the CAPM in rate-of-return testimony estimate beta by statistical analysis of realized rates of return on common stock relative to realized rates of return on an index of the stock market, such as the Standard & Poor's composite index. Monthly stock returns over the last five years are the most commonly used data base for estimating betas. A number of investment services now routinely report betas. Beta is estimated by a least-squares regression of stock returns on market returns. The estimated slope coefficient of this regression is a measure of beta. Some variations, such as giving more weight to more recent data, exist.[31]

A witness or an investment service (such as *Value Line Investment Survey*) may report "adjusted" betas. While the details of the adjustment may vary, the effect is to move betas above or below one slightly closer to one. Two justifications have been offered for the need to adjust betas. One is that empirical studies of how betas change over time show that betas tend to "regress" toward one (see Blume 1971 and 1975). The other is a "Bayesian" justification, that one knows the *average* beta to be one, so adjusting an estimated beta toward one is an appropriate use of prior information (see Vasicek 1973). Whether such adjustments are appropriate is an unresolved question.

r_f. In the CAPM theory, the risk-free rate is the rate of return investors can realize with certainty. Its nearest analog is the yield on short-term United States government securities, such as ninety-day Treasury bills. However, in rate-of-return testimony a longer maturity government bond rate is often substituted. The rationale for this substitution is not always clearly stated. It may be an attempt to forecast the average Treasury bill rate over the period for which rates are to be set. It may also be an attempt to smooth out fluctuations in the cost of capital.[32]

$[E(r_m) - r_f]$. The figure most often used for the market-risk premium is about 8 percent, based on work by Ibbotson and Sinquefield 1982. The assumptions implicit in this estimate are explored by Merton 1980, who investigates alternative assumptions as well. Using the data base employed by Ibbotson and Sinquefield,[33] Merton obtains estimates of the market-risk premium ranging from 8 to 12 percent based on alternative assumptions.

The Ibbotson and Sinquefield results are based on fifty-six years of actual stock returns. Returns over a much shorter period, five or ten years, are sometimes used to compute the market-risk premium. This is a serious mistake because the return on the stock market is so volatile that the standard deviation for the mean market return over any short period is very large. Results of an estimate derived from such a short period are inadequate.

The return on a share of common stock comes in two forms: capital gains $(P_t - P_{t-1})$ and dividends, D_t. The one-period rate of return, r_t, is equal to the return divided by the beginning-of-period price:

$$r_t = (P_t - P_{t-1})/P_{t-1} + D_t/P_{t-1}$$
$$= (P_t + D_t)/P_{t-1} - 1.$$

The beta coefficient can be estimated by an ordinary least-squares regression of $(r_j - r_f)$ on $(r_m - r_f)$, the realized returns on the stock and the market in each period, as just computed.[34] When this procedure is applied to the stock and market returns in table 3.5, the estimated beta coefficient is 0.81. (In practice, one would use many more observations in order to obtain a reliable estimate of beta; five years of monthly data—sixty observations—is common practice.)[35]

The historical risk premium on the Standard & Poor's 500 common stocks calculated by Ibbotson and Sinquefield 1982 is frequently used as an estimate of the expected market-risk premium. The mean excess return (common stocks minus Treasury bills) from 1926 to 1981 was 8.3 percent per annum.

Note that the *arithmetic* mean, *not* the geometric mean, is the rele-

Table 3.5
Simplified example: Capital Asset Pricing Model (CAPM) method

Month/year	Closing price	Capital gain	Dividends per share	Yield	Stock return	Market return[a]
12/76	$19 4/8	—	$0	0	—	—
1/77	23 7/8	.2244	0	0	.2244	−.0489
2/77	25 4/8	.0681	0.20	.0084	.0764	−.0151
3/77	22 6/8	−.1078	0	0	−.1078	−.0119
4/77	25 7/8	.1374	0	0	.1374	.0014
5/77	26 3/8	.0193	0.20	.0077	.0271	−.0150
6/77	31	.1754	0	0	.1754	.0475
7/77	30 4/8	−.0161	0	0	−.0161	−.0151
8/77	28 4/8	−.0656	0.20	.0066	−.0590	−.0133
9/77	34 3/8	.2061	0	0	.2061	.0000
10/77	32 5/8	−.0509	0	0	−.0509	−.0415
11/77	34 7/8	.0690	0.25	.0077	.0766	.0370
12/77	33 1/8	−.0502	0	0	−.0502	.0048

[a]From 1977 Summary Update Sheet to Ibbotson and Sinquefield 1977, total return on common stock series.

vant value for this purpose. The quantity desired is the rate of return that investors expect over the next year for the random annual rate of return on the market. The arithmetic mean, or simple average, is the unbiased measure of the expected value of repeated observations of a random variable, not the geometric mean.[36] The geometric mean is less than the arithmetic mean (unless all years' actual rates of return are the same) and therefore underestimates the expected annual rate of return.[37]

To combine these components into an estimate of the cost of equity, suppose that the yield on a new government note maturing two years hence is 13.0 percent.[38] Given 8.3 percent and 0.81 as our best estimates of the expected market-risk premium and the beta coefficient, this implies that the CAPM estimate of the cost of equity over the next two years is:

$$E(r_j) = 13.0 + (0.81)(8.3) = 19.7\%.$$

Logical Consistency and Consistency with Theory

The CAPM is logically consistent. If its assumptions are valid, regulators using it with appropriate data will measure the cost of capital. Moreover, the risk-free rate and the market-risk premium are clearly independent of actions by regulators. While the company's risk (and therefore its beta) might be influenced by regulatory actions, there is little chance that a commission's decision to use the method would automatically create serious biases in the data needed to use the method in the following proceeding.

The CAPM is also generally consistent with modern finance theory. Its assumptions are not automatically violated by changes in broad economic forces (such as a new rate of inflation) or by regulatory actions. Nonetheless, the CAPM has been criticized both as a theory and as a method for use in rate-of-return hearings. The most serious criticisms for ratemaking purposes make one of two charges: (1) the CAPM theory is wrong in a way that invalidates equation (3.11), the CAPM risk-return line shown in figure 3.3; or (2) while equation (3.11) may be acceptable, the quantities needed to apply it cannot be estimated with enough precision to make the method useful.

Criticisms of CAPM Theory

Most of the analysis of the CAPM theory focuses on whether a stock's beta with respect to the market is truly sufficient to judge relative risk—are other risk factors needed?[39] A number of such factors have been proposed, and the empirical evidence testing these theories is mixed. Nevertheless, if there is another factor, we have to add *something* to the basic CAPM equation.

The something most often added is alpha, α. That is, equation (3.11) is replaced by

$$E(r_j) = r_f + \alpha_j + \{\beta_j \times [E(r_m) - r_f]\}. \tag{3.12}$$

If the *expected* value of alpha[40] is not equal to zero, then the CAPM is an incomplete model. That is, a positive or negative *ex ante* alpha represents any part of the cost of capital unrelated to the "market" factor. If we knew a way to predict alpha in advance, we would be able to improve on the estimates of the pure CAPM.

Several factors might justify the inclusion of alpha, including:[41]

1. Company size, since there is evidence that investors in small companies require higher rates of return than predicted by the CAPM. Thus one might include a positive alpha for very small firms.[42]
2. Dividend policy, because of differential personal tax rates on dividends and capital gains. High-payout firms would have positive alphas.[43]
3. Unique risk, measured by the standard deviation of returns, because investors may be incompletely diversified.
4. Asymmetry in the distribution of returns, because investors might prefer stocks where the possibility of a very large gain is greater than the possibility of a very large loss, and conversely.[44]

These are unresolved issues in finance. Whether one adjusts the pure CAPM estimate to reflect one or more of these factors is a matter of judgment. As always, witnesses who make such adjustments should be expected to explain their decisions.

Criticisms of CAPM Applications

Some critics assert that the quantities needed to apply the CAPM cannot be estimated with enough precision to make the method useful. Examples of this type of criticism include the following.

The return on the market, r_m, and the market-risk premium, $E[(r_m) - r_f]$, are supposed to be based on *all* assets, not just a stock market index such as the Standard & Poor's 500. Even a perfect stock market index excludes a wide range of assets, such as precious metals, residential real estate, bonds, and many others. Roll 1977 argues that

CAPM tests are useless unless the *right* market index is found; and since there is no way of testing whether available indexes are good enough proxies (lacking the right index), the CAPM is not a valid operational theory. In other words, even if the CAPM were valid, there is no practical way to assemble the data needed to use such a model.[45]

Critics also note that estimates of beta using historical data may not be sufficiently reliable estimates of current betas. Even if there has been no change in the business or financial risks of the firm, one may still challenge the statistical accuracy of beta estimates. This issue can be dealt with fairly easily. The statistics that accompany the estimation of beta give a direct indication of the range of possible error. Also, betas for portfolios of stocks are likely to be more reliable than betas for individual stocks.

If there is reason to believe that the *systematic* risks of the firm or industry have changed, however, historical estimates of beta face the same problems that any of the cost-of-capital estimation methods would face in such circumstances. Historical betas must be used with caution.

Another potential problem is that the market-risk premium may be changing over time. Applications of the CAPM usually rely on works such as those by Ibbotson and Sinquefield 1982 and Holland and Myers 1979 and 1980, which focus on average returns over long periods. The required risk premium may vary in the short run, but it is difficult or impossible to measure such variations.

If these long-period estimates are correct, short-run fluctuations around them should cancel out over time. Therefore CAPM estimates can be right on average even if wrong on a "spot" basis. Of course, any method relying on historical data may also be affected if the market risk premium is temporarily high or low; such a condition implies problems for most methods, not just for the CAPM.

Merton 1980 focused on a different problem: whether the assumptions used in obtaining the long-run estimates of the market-risk premium are important. He showed that different and equally plausible assumptions about investor attitudes yield long-run estimates of the market-risk premium that vary between 8 and 12 percent, compared to Ibbotson and Sinquefield's 9 percent. (Merton does not show that the Ibbotson and Sinquefield assumptions are wrong, only that plausible alternative assumptions give different answers.) The potential for this problem has long been known, but it was not known to cause so large a difference.

One Response to the Criticisms: The "Empirical" CAPM
These and similar criticisms have stimulated a number of variations of the CAPM theory. One is to focus directly on what capital market data actually reveal rather than to include all the possible theoretical effects in more elaborate equations. This approach was taken by Litzenberger, Ramaswamy, and Sosin 1980 (LRS), who provide both a useful summary of the criticisms of the CAPM and their importance for rate-of-return hearings and econometric estimates of the combined importance of a number of these effects in an "empirical" CAPM equation.

The LRS conclusions are based on their econometric estimates of a model that approximately corrects for a number of CAPM criticisms. Their estimates yield a line based on historical data that has a lower slope and a higher intercept than the CAPM theory predicts (see figure 3.4). Based on this historical relationship, LRS conclude that applications of the standard CAPM that use only New York Stock

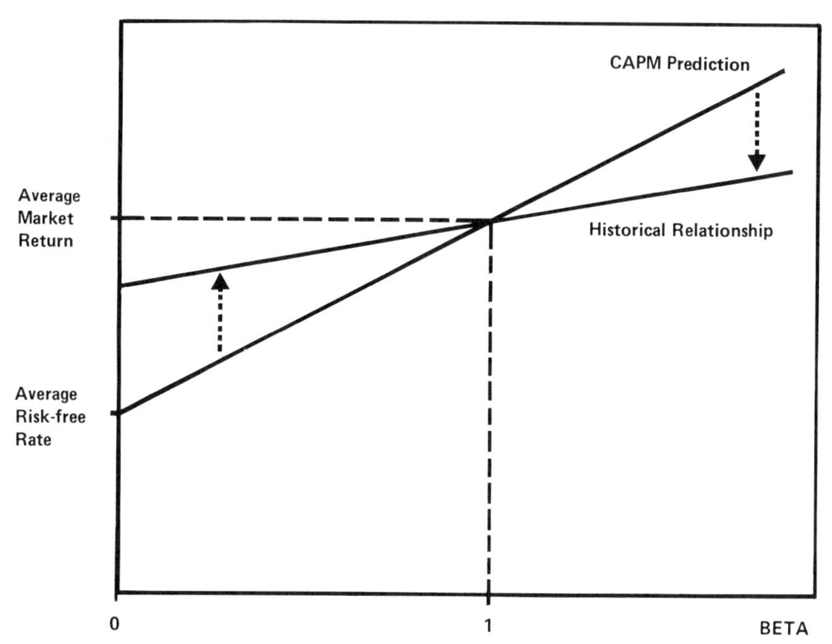

Figure 3.4
Long-Run Relationship between Average Returns and Beta

Exchange assets to compute betas will underestimate (or overestimate) the cost of capital for firms having (1) an NYSE beta less than (or greater than) one; (2) a dividend yield that is higher (or lower) than that of the average NYSE stock; and/or (3) negatively (or positively) skewed returns. If so, the standard CAPM will tend to underestimate the required rates of return for most utilities, primarily because utilities tend to have betas less than one.

This work appears well done and the results are intuitively appealing, but more research on how much the LRS econometric estimates change over time is in order. If the estimates prove stable in future tests, their method may become a useful approach in rate-of-return hearings.

Implications of the Criticisms

Many of the criticisms of the CAPM theory and its empirical applications appear to have merit, although final returns on the validity of the CAPM as a theory are not yet in. Our feeling is that the criticisms do not imply that the CAPM should not be used; rather, like any other cost-of-capital estimation method, it should be used carefully. Despite the criticisms it is clear that: (1) the CAPM is not fundamentally inconsistent with current understanding of how capital markets work; (2) beta is an important indicator of relative risk, even if it may not be the only risk indicator that matters; and (3) a cost-of-capital estimate made using the CAPM is likely to provide useful information.

Moreover, the relevant comparison for the CAPM is not against some unknown "correct" method but against the other methods actually in use. The long list of potential criticisms of the CAPM may exist because the CAPM addresses explicitly a number of issues that other methods sweep under the rug. Many witnesses will prefer variations of the original CAPM; but the pure CAPM is far less sensitive to factors that create serious problems for the more widely used CE and DCF approaches.[46] We think the criticisms of the CAPM should be used as a way to improve the CAPM estimates rather than an excuse to discard the method.

Data Requirements and the Method's Costs

The basic CAPM requires an amount of data roughly equivalent to that needed for the DCF approach and equally available. Estimates of beta can be obtained from several investment services (the *Value Line Investment Survey* and the Merrill Lynch *Security Risk Evaluation Service*, for example) or calculated directly from security market data. Values for the risk-free rate and estimates of the market-risk premium are readily available, although the "true" value of the latter is unobservable. More complicated versions of the CAPM typically involve more complicated analysis of the same data, not more data. The CAPM scores at least as well as DCF on data requirements—somewhat better in volatile times because it is less sensitive to some sources of volatility, such as changes in inflation and interest rates.

The CAPM is the most recent major method to emerge. It is the basic paradigm used most in capital market theory, so both the theory and the empirical results that make use of it are continually evolving. The statistical tools used in CAPM applications are often complex and sophisticated; the associated costs and difficulty are probably the highest of the five methods we have considered in detail. Nonetheless some commissions have decided to use the CAPM and apparently find the related costs acceptable.

5. Risk Positioning

Risk Positioning, also called the "risk premium" method, is less widely used as a stand-alone method but is often used to supplement other evidence. Risk Positioning is likely to be especially appealing in periods with significant changes in broad capital market conditions, for instance, when there are numerous shifts in the market risk-return line, as illustrated in figure 2.3.

Definition and Example

Risk Positioning (RP) is in some ways the least well defined of the methods we evaluate in detail. A variety of procedures might come under this label, many including a substantial dollop of "expert judgment." As used here, RP implies that the recommended rate of return is found by adding an explicit premium for risk to a current interest rate, usually to the interest rate on government bonds. Methods of determining this risk premium vary.

Some experts rely on their general knowledge and experience, combined with evidence on the risk premium on other assets. A witness might cite the Ibbotson and Sinquefield data to estimate that the average stock requires a risk premium of about 9 percent, decide the stock of this company is less risky than average, and pick 7 percent to add to a current market interest rate. An application of this type will often be used to check the results of other approaches.

Other experts may use far more elaborate ways to estimate the required risk premium. Sometimes DCF and CAPM estimates are just part of the initial evidence the witness uses in selecting a risk premium. Other measures, including the standard deviation of the stock's rate of return and the company's bond rating, may also be considered.

The fundamental premise underlying all RP applications is that shifts in the interest rate the witness selects will shift the height of the risk-return line without having a significant effect on the required risk premium.

As an example, suppose a witness believes that the cost of equity is equal to interest rate on long-term government bonds plus a premium that reflects the risk of the utility in question. The current interest rate (yield to maturity) on long-term government bonds can be observed directly. The expected excess rate of return on common stocks over long-term government bonds might be estimated by reference to the historical returns on two portfolios: a large portfolio of common stocks and another portfolio of long-term government bonds.

To illustrate the latter calculation, let r_{st} equal the realized rate of return on the common stock portfolio in year t. Let r_{bt} equal the realized rate of return on the long-term government bond portfolio in year t. Then an estimate of the risk premium, PRE, on common stocks measured with respect to government bonds is given by the mean annual difference in returns on the two portfolios over an n year period:

$$PRE = \Sigma(r_{st} - r_{bt})/n. \tag{3.13}$$

Suppose the current interest rate on long-term government bonds is 13.5 percent.[47] The witness has gone through the exercise embodied in (3.13) (or has used the results of other researchers, such as Ibbotson and Sinquefield), and computes the historical risk premium on common stocks measured with respect to long-term government bonds as 8.3 percent. Moreover, the witness asserts that the utility in question is equal in risk to the average common stock. Then the cost of equity for firm j at time t estimated by this application of the risk-positioning method is just

$$r_{jt} = r_{bt} + PRE \tag{3.14}$$

$$= 13.5 + 8.3 = 21.8\%.$$

This is a simple application of the RP approach. The risk premium calculation can be far more sophisticated, perhaps using the CAPM risk premium (i.e., $\beta_j \times [E(r_m) - r_f]$) only as a first step in the selection of a final risk premium. Also, another interest rate might be chosen. Regardless of the complexity of the calculation of PRE and the interest rate, however, the final step in the RP method is to use an equation like (3.14) to calculate the required rate of return.

Logical Consistency and Consistency with Theory

The logical consistency of the RP approach is sound, providing that circular methods are avoided in setting the required risk premium. Given the assumptions, an RP estimate aims at finding the cost of capital. As usually applied the method has no obvious mechanism by which a commission's action this time could bias the data needed next time. One exception is if the firm's own debt cost is used as the interest rate.

Some witnesses believe that the risk premium over the company's own current interest rate on bonds is the appropriate way to apply the RP approach. This can lead to a circularity problem. Suppose a company must pay 14 percent for new debt. The company's commission adopts the RP approach, sets *PRE* equal to 5 percent, and grants an allowed rate of return on equity of 19 percent. This improves the company's finances, so its cost of new debt falls to 13.5 percent. At the next hearing, the commission uses the same estimate of *PRE* and arrives at an equity cost of 18.5 percent instead of 19 percent.

The problem is that the cost of equity to the company need not have fallen by 0.5 percent just because the company's cost of debt has. The commission's use of the company's own debt cost, which is affected by the commission's actions, can affect the data needed in the cost-of-equity estimation procedure.

This problem is likely to be minor relative to the other uncertainties in estimating the cost of equity, because interest rates on corporate bonds do not vary nearly as much as the cost of equity.[48] Compare the 0.5-percentage-point difference in this example with the range of 13.9

to 21.2 percent in the DCF estimates of the cost of equity—caused by different choices of a growth rate estimation method—in the DCF simplified example.

The RP approach's consistency with current theory varies according to the procedures used by a particular witness and the care with which they are applied. All applications raise the following general question: Is it reasonable to assume that important changes in interest rates signal changes in the *height* of the market risk-return line, without changing the *slope* of the line (i.e., the premium for a given degree of risk)?

In principle, the slope of the market line will change whenever the factors that determine the market risk premium change. Unfortunately, there is no generally accepted way to measure these factors or to quantify how they change over time.[49] As a practical matter there is little alternative to using a constant premium for ratemaking purposes.[50]

The practical difficulties with measuring the market-risk premium do not imply that the potential for changes should be ignored. Two specific issues are worth consideration. First, some interest rates are more vulnerable to problems than others. Second, inflation is sometimes cited as a reason that the risk premium for utility stocks is low or even negative.

Interest Rate Selection

On conceptual grounds, some interest rates are more likely to be vulnerable to the possibility of changing risk premiums than others. Specifically, the risk premium of stocks over corporate bonds is more vulnerable than the risk premium of stocks over federal government bonds. Government securities are therefore generally preferable to corporate securities in selecting the interest rate for an RP application.

One reason the use of corporate bonds can lead to additional problems is that they often contain call provisions that are valuable to the borrower. If interest rates are high, lenders probably demand a "call premium" on such bonds as compensation for the chance that the company will redeem the bonds early if interest rates come down. Call provisions on government bonds, however, are typically restricted to the last five years before maturity, which is far more favorable to lenders. Government bonds are therefore less likely to contain significant call premiums, which can obscure the long-term relationship between returns on stocks and bonds.

ognize this volatility. The fact that the RP technique and the CAPM do so automatically is an *advantage* of these methods.

Put another way, the Comparable Earnings and DCF techniques may be less responsive to current capital market conditions and less likely to result in high and variable rates of return. But that is a disadvantage in trying to measure the nominal cost of capital in times when it is high and variable.[53]

The real problem for regulators is less whether to rely on a method that is sensitive to current conditions than how rapidly to try to adjust the rate of return to the current cost of capital. This issue is not one of measurement but of basic regulatory methodology.[54]

Since regulatory procedures, not the estimation technique, are responsible for the alleged problem, we give the RP technique a good score on the related cost criterion.[55]

6. Market-to-Book Ratio

The Market-to-Book Ratio (MBR) method is also relatively new. It is preferred by a few witnesses but is not widely used by commissions.

Definition and Example

The MBR approach is grounded on the premise that the market value of a company's stock should equal book value, and will do so if the allowed rate of return equals the cost of capital.[56] We concluded earlier that this premise is sound. Although the underlying concept is sensible, its application is not as straightforward as it appears.

The market-to-book ratio can be used to estimate the cost of capital in two ways.

The first is to adjust this company's rate of return depending on this company's market-to-book ratio. For example, if the current allowed rate of return were 12 percent, the market-to-book ratio 0.75, and investors expect the 12 percent to persist indefinitely, the cost of capital is $12/.75 = 16$ percent. This works because under these assumptions, $(M/B) = (ROR/r)$, where ROR is the allowed rate of return and r is the cost of capital. Therefore, $r = ROR/(M/B)$. This kind of simple application is more often used as a check on other results than as a stand-alone method, for reasons discussed later.

The second approach relies on statistical analysis of the market-to-book ratios of a number of companies and is used as a stand-alone method. Formal applications of the MBR method usually follow this second approach. The analyst fits a statistical equation to explain the market-to-book ratios of a sample of regulated firms. The explanatory variables include allowed and/or earned rates of return as well as various measures or proxies for risk.

The form of the equation is

$$\frac{M}{B} = a_0 + (a_1 \times ROR) + (a_2 \times V_2) + \ldots + (a_N \times V_N), \qquad (3.15)$$

which says that the market-to-book ratio of a firm equals the sum of several factors, including a constant, a_0, an *effect* of allowed or earned rate of return, a_1, times the allowed or earned rate of return, *ROR*, and the effects of other variables times the values of those variables for a given firm.

A least-squares regression procedure provides estimates of the variables' effects (i.e., of the a_ns) using the market-to-book ratios and other variable values, including allowed or earned rates of return, for a sample of companies over some historical period. Using the estimates obtained from the regression for the parameter values of equation (3.15), the analyst solves for the allowed rate of return that makes the market-to-book ratio equal one.[57] This allowed rate is the method's estimate of the cost of capital.

To implement the MBR as a stand-alone method, the analyst selects a set of variables including rate of return and market-to-book ratio, and analyzes them statistically. Suppose allowed rates of return, *ROR*, betas, and debt ratios, *DR*, are collected for a sample of forty electric utilities. Suppose the equation that best fits these data, with parameters estimated using ordinary least-squares regression, is:

$$\frac{M}{B} = 0.37 + 8.0\ ROR - 0.5\ beta - 0.91\ DR.$$

The problem is to set the proper allowed rate for Transylvania Electric. Suppose this firm's beta is $beta = 0.65$ and its debt ratio is $DR = 0.53$. Then we can solve the fitted equation for the level of *ROR* that makes Transylvania Electric's market-to-book ratio equal to one:

$$\frac{M}{B} = 1.0 = 0.37 + 8.0\ ROR - 0.5\ beta - 0.91\ DR,$$

$$= 0.37 + 8.0\ ROR - 0.5(0.65) - 0.91(0.53),$$

implying,

$$ROR = \frac{[1.0 - 0.37 + 0.5(0.65) + 0.91(0.53)]}{8.0}$$

$$= 0.1797 = 18\%.$$

If the fitted equation works for Transylvania Electric, and the goal is a market-to-book ratio of one, the allowed rate of return should be about 18 percent.

Logical Consistency and Consistency with Theory

The MBR approach has difficulty achieving logical consistency. The procedure does aim at finding the cost of capital, but a commission's use of the method tends to bias the data (the market price of stocks) needed to use the method next time. This is most serious if the stock price of the firm in question in used, as with the first of the two MBR approaches. This bias can be overcome by a very mechanical application of the first MBR approach but otherwise creates serious problems. Similar problems arise for the second MBR approach.

To explain these problems, we first suppose that the commission does *not* use the fitted equation just described but instead uses the first MBR approach. Suppose Transylvania Electric's current allowed return is ($ROR = 0.12$) and its market-to-book ratio is ($M/B = 0.9$). The commission might conclude that the current rate of return is 90 percent of the firm's cost of capital, since the market-to-book ratio is 90 percent of the desired level of one. This works if investors expect no regulatory actions.

But suppose the market-to-book ratio is now 0.9 because investors *expect* the regulators to increase the allowed rate of return to 90 percent of the true cost of capital (e.g., to 16.2 percent, which is 90 percent of 18 percent). Then the increase to $[12 \times (1.0/0.9)] = 13.3$ percent will dash their hopes; the market-to-book ratio will *fall*, not rise, when the new allowed rate is announced.

The problem is that Transylvania Electric's current market-to-book ratio is largely determined by what investors expect regulators to do. That ratio is therefore not a useful statistic for Transylvania's regulators, unless regulators know exactly what investors expect.

Stand-alone applications of the MBR approach (the second version of the MBR method, as illustrated in the simplified example) use data for a sample of firms in the same industry. This may avoid the circularity problem just described, since Transylvania's regulators do not use Transylvania's stock price in their calculations. Several cases should be distinguished.

Suppose that other firms' allowed rates of return are *not* expected to change. Then firms that are earning their cost of capital *now* will be selling at market-to-book ratios equal to one. Firms earning more or less than the cost of capital will sell at ratios more or less than one. The statistical analysis will reveal the fair rate of return for the industry. Transylvania's regulators could use this return without logical consistency problems, at least at first.

However, suppose other regulators are expected to change allowed returns in the near future. The market prices of these firms' stocks reflect the rates of return investors *expect* to be granted not the rate of return allowed today. The actual market-to-book ratio will be higher than justified by today's returns, so the coefficient of *ROR* will be too high in the estimated market-to-book equation. If Transylvania's regulators use this coefficient, they underestimate the required rate of return.

If the coefficient of the returns investors actually expect is 8.0, as in the above example, but the coefficient of today's returns is 10.0,[58] when Transylvania's regulators solve (3.15) for the required rate of return, they calculate,

$$ROR = [1.0 - 0.37 + 0.5(0.65) + 0.91(0.53)]/10.0,$$

$$= 0.1437,$$

or 14.4 percent. Investors, who require 18 percent, are again disappointed, and Transylvania's market-to-book ratio stays below one.

Finally, suppose other regulators use the MBR method also. Suppose no rate hearings are scheduled, so it would be reasonable to expect today's rate of return to persist for a while, but suppose also that the market-to-book ratios for some of these companies are below one. Investors might anticipate that the company could successfully petition for a rate increase, since regulators rely on the market-to-book ratio. Investors would then expect higher returns to occur sooner than before, driving up the market-to-book ratio and again biasing the statistical results in an MBR equation. Regulators are back in the same circle as when they used Transylvania's own stock price.

The basic problem is that *ROR* in (3.15) should be *expected ROR* if the second MBR approach is to work. If the *ROR* used in the statistical procedure differs from expected *ROR* for the companies in the statistical sample, the MBR method gives the wrong answer.

In principle, such problems can be avoided if the commission applies the first version of the MBR method in a very mechanical way. The commission must spell out its exact procedures in advance and then stick to those procedures no matter what happens. The market price can be exactly interpreted in this case. We will give an artificial and unrealistic example to illustrate the logical point.

The commission estimates the cost of capital as well as it can and announces that this rate of return will persist for exactly one year (or for any fixed period of its choice). After that time the commission will adjust the rate of return to equate market and book value. The expected earnings stream of the stock is then known exactly by investors: it will earn the rate of return times the rate base the first year, and then could be sold for a value equal to the rate base. That is, the market value of the stock would be equal to[59]

$$M_0 = \frac{(D_1)}{\sqrt{(1 + r)}} + \frac{RB_1}{(1 + r)} \tag{3.16}$$

which says the market value at the start of the year will equal the value of dividends expected during the year, discounted for the six months' average delay in getting the dividends, plus the value of the rate base at the end of the year, discounted for the year's delay. The rate base at year's end will reflect the division of this year's allowed earnings between dividends and retained earnings.

Immediately after the announcement, the stock price will reflect the market's view of the value of the stock under this procedure, M_0. This new price could be used in (3.16) to solve for r, the cost of capital the market requires. Investors might be skeptical at first. If so, the initial market value will be too low and the implied cost of capital too high. But if the procedure is to work the commission must stick to it nonetheless. Investors will be convinced of the commission's resolve only if it is demonstrated. Eventually, such a procedure would make rate-of-return determination automatic.

This procedure is not circular, since the allowed rate of return depends on the market's view of the worth of the announced rate of return; the market provides an independent check, and will signal a too-high rate by a market value well in excess of book value. It may also be worth noting that the procedure does not make the investment riskless; expected returns, not actual returns, are set. The firm is just as likely to do better or worse after the fact as it is today. If the procedure did reduce the risk the market perceives (move the firm down the risk-return line as illustrated in figure 2.3), the market price would be higher and the cost of capital lower. The long-run benefits of any resulting reduction in risk would automatically go to ratepayers in the form of lower capital costs. To the extent that current procedures have resulted in capital losses for existing investors by setting rates of return too low, these losses would be reversed. That is, the procedure would reverse any gains and losses from a previous decision to not set the rate of return equal to the cost of capital.

This procedure is offered as an illustration of the logical difficulties with the MBR method and not as a proposed remedy for the rate-of-return problem. The real issue is that the MBR method *as currently applied* will work only as long as today's rates of return are expected to persist and the market does not know that commissions are using the market-to-book ratio. New application procedures are necessary if commissions begin to rely on the MBR approach.

Most of our discussion here has focused on the logical consistency of the MBR method, but completeness requires that two issues regarding the method's consistency with theory also be addressed: the validity of the premise that a market-to-book ratio of one implies an expected rate of return equal to the cost of capital, and the validity of the procedures used to implement this premise. We addressed the first issue in chapter 2 and concluded that the premise is sound. The problems are found in the second issue.

The estimated coefficients (the a_ns) in equation (3.15) depend on the *ROR* in the data being the *ROR* investors expect. Even if true initially this can change if commissions begin to use the method. These coefficients are reliable for setting rates of return in ratemaking hearings only as long as today's *ROR*s are "sticky," which in part implies investors do not believe commissions are using the procedure to adjust *ROR*s when the market-to-book ratio falls below one.

This is the most fundamental problem with current applications of the MBR but it is not the only one. The other variables in (3.15) sometimes are included with minimal theoretical justification, based solely on how well they predict the market-to-book ratios in a particular sample of data. By random chance, such "kitchen sink" regressions will find some factors to be significant when they actually are irrelevant. Predictions based on such chance correlations may not be accurate.

As illustrated by the example of a mechanical application of the MBR, the need for any form of empirical equation such as (3.15) is questionable, except as an aid in the initial setting of the allowed rate of return. If the MBR approach is to be used consistently, regulators must be able to interpret the market price. For this to be possible, investors must be able to predict regulators' actions (or at least commissions must know what investors are predicting). In the long run, the only way this condition can be met consistently is if regulators pick a set of rules and follow them mechanically. The resulting feedback between the commission's use of the method and the market's reaction to that use is likely to make equation (3.15) irrelevant after its initial application.

Data Requirements and the Method's Costs

Because implementation procedures vary so much, the data requirements of the MBR method are difficult to assess. Stock prices and allowed rates of return are readily observable and objective, but the true variable needed (*expected* rates of return) is unobservable except in mechanical applications. Since the other variables in the regression equation vary from case to case, it also is conceivable that there would be additional discrepancies between the observed and needed variables; this can only be judged case by case.

The method is not widely used and so may require some additional explanation. However, the underlying premise is widely known and the applications tend not to be especially complicated. Of the less used methods, MBR scores well on related costs.

7. Conclusions from the Conceptual Evaluation

The conceptual evaluation does not produce a clear "winner" among the five methods but does suggest that some have far more serious problems than others.

Comparable Earnings

There are serious problems with the Comparable Earnings method. Only by chance will conventional application of comparable earnings yield an estimate of the rate of return equal to the cost of capital. Furthermore, the difference between this estimate and the cost of capital is likely to be significant. The CE method scores quite poorly on most conceptual criteria and it is clearly the worst of the five methods examined in detail.

In fairness it should be noted that an expert may sometimes use the CE method as a rough guide to his or her judgment and experience or as a supplement to the results of other methods. In such applications, the end result of the witness's testimony could turn out to be reasonable if the expert is skilled and aware of the problems with the CE approach, and the commission could find the testimony helpful. The problem is that the true evidence in such testimony would be the skill of the expert or the results of the other methods, not the CE results on which the witness's recommendation apparently rests.

While the evidence of a witness using the CE method should not be rejected out of hand, the witness should be expected to address seriously the many problems with CE raised in this chapter.

Discounted Cash Flow

The DCF method is conceptually sound when the stable conditions on which it relies actually exist. When conditions differ because of broad factors such as inflation, it is usually possible to predict at least the direction of bias in a DCF calculation. Also, it may be possible to vary the calculations used in the method to accommodate variable rates of inflation, by estimating the real rather than nominal growth rate of dividends.

If the business or financial risks of the company have changed, it will be difficult to adjust the DCF estimate to current conditions. On balance the DCF score is substantially better than that of CE but still mixed on the conceptual criteria.

Capital Asset Pricing Model

Of the three well-defined methods reviewed (CE, DCF, and CAPM), the CAPM has the best score on consistency with theory and the worst on related costs. The method also scores well on logical consistency and data requirements.

Despite its high score on consistency with theory, the CAPM is not the final word on the theoretical determinants of the cost of capital, and many witnesses will prefer variations of the CAPM that overcome some of the criticisms made of it. Good cases can be made for some of these variations, and a witness's testimony is likely to be most helpful if it presents more than the results from the basic CAPM alone.

Risk Positioning

The RP method is hard to define because of the variations in how the risk premium is found. Essentially, it makes the CAPM tradeoff between consistency with theory and related costs into an option. Through choice of the method of finding the risk premium, witnesses and commissions can select different combinations of theoretical accuracy and costs to achieve that accuracy. Barring some strange way of finding the risk premium (and use of the company's own cost of debt, which causes only a minor problem) the method is logically consistent. Data requirements vary with the details of the calculation. Overall, the RP technique scores well on the conceptual evaluation.

Market-to-Book Ratio

The premise underlying the MBR approach is sound and could be used to set rates of return if the procedures were carefully designed and implemented. But the MBR technique *as used* fails the test of logical consistency, and for similar reasons scores poorly on consistency with theory. The method does reasonably well on the practical criteria of data requirements and related costs. Its score is lowered significantly by its potential for circularity.

We are not yet ready to summarize the overall performance of the five principal methods. The conceptual evaluation relies on only four of the six evaluative criteria described at the outset of the chapter. The next chapter completes the evaluation of the five principal methods with an empirical analysis of the methods' performance and concludes with a table summarizing the overall results of the evaluation.

4 The Five Major Methods: Empirical Evaluation and Overall Rankings

Our empirical evaluation consists chiefly of analysis of a sample of regulated and unregulated companies to examine some important properties of cost-of-equity estimation methods. The chapter also briefly summarizes published data on the various methods favored by regulatory agencies, not to imply that methods are either good or bad, but only that regulators, for whatever reason, have found some more useful than others.

1. Empirical Evaluation

Approach Used to Infer Accuracy of Methods

It is not possible to test directly the accuracy of different methods for determining the cost of equity. To do so would require knowledge of the true cost of equity. But if we knew the true cost of equity, our task—and that of the regulator—would be trivial. Therefore, we must rely on indirect tests. Instead of asking whether a method accurately estimates the cost of capital, we ask: Does it have sensible properties when observed over time? Four questions pinpoint these properties:

1. Does the estimated cost of equity respond to changes in market interest rates?
2. How do the predictions of alternative models compare?
3. Are the parameters of each method stable?
4. How sensitive are cost-of-equity estimates to minor changes in estimation methods?

Before proceeding with analysis of these properties, a possible objection should be dealt with. Specifically, some readers will think of the following simple test: compare the estimated cost of equity to the realized rate of return. The method that does the best job of predicting returns is judged superior. In effect, the average *realized* rate of return is used as an estimate of the *expected* rate of return, and the method is tested on how well it matches this estimate.

The problem with this test is that the mean realized rate of return is an imprecise estimate of the expected rate of return. As long as the expected rate of return is stable over the sample period, the mean rate of return is an unbiased estimate of the expected rate of return. Bias is not the main problem. The problem lies in the precision of the estimate. Common stock returns are extremely volatile. Even if we observe the realized rate of return for a period of many years, the variance of the estimate is very large; therefore the estimate offers little power as a test of how well a method works.

This problem can be demonstrated by an example. Ibbotson and Sinquefield 1982 calculated the mean annual return on the Standard & Poor's Composite Index from 1926 to 1981, a period of fifty-six years. This index consisted of ninety common stocks until 1957 and five hundred common stocks since then. The mean value was 11.4 percent. The standard deviation of the annual return was 21.9 percent. A 95-percent confidence interval for the mean return of the distribution underlying this sample (i.e., for the expected rate of return on the Standard & Poor index) is 11.4 ± 5.9 percent,[1] a wide interval considering the large number of stocks and long sample period. Tests of predicted returns against actual returns are likely to founder on the extreme variability of actual returns.

We will not evaluate all five methods discussed in the previous chapter. We will evaluate the CE method, the DCF model, and the CAPM. The earnings-price ratio method, a variant of the DCF model, is also examined. The risk positioning method (RP) is not evaluated because it is not a precisely defined methodology. (Notice, however, that with respect to one of the empirical evaluation criteria the RP method performs very well: a consistently applied RP estimate of the cost of equity will move with interest rates automatically.) Like the RP method, the market-to-book ratio method is not precisely defined. Lacking a standardized set of variables in the MBR equation, we cannot be sure that any particular implementation will represent the method fairly. Furthermore, the extreme logical consistency problems with this method suggested that we not pursue it here.

The data used in this analysis come from a sample of 136 publicly traded companies. These companies were grouped into eleven industries using the two-digit SIC code. One group is composed of electric utilities; the remaining groups are unregulated companies. A description of the sample and other technical notes on the empirical analysis are in appendix C.[2]

Responsiveness to Interest Rates and Comparison among Estimates

Since the cost of equity is determined in the capital markets, it is natural to look there for evidence of changes in capital costs. Although the cost of equity cannot be observed directly, it is possible to observe the yields on various debt instruments.[3] Some of the same factors that affect the cost of debt also affect the cost of equity. One way to test cost-of-equity estimation methods is to see how well they follow changes in interest rates. In doing so we end up comparing the methods with one another (the second of the four tests) as well.

Approach

We used the following procedure. A recent historical test period was selected. At periodic intervals during this test period, we estimated the cost of equity using each of the alternative methods. We plotted these estimates on a graph against contemporaneous interest rates for comparison. The precise test period and estimation interval are not crucial. We require only that the period contain some variability of interest rates, since we are not likely to learn much if interest rates are constant. For convenience, we selected the period from 1971 to 1980; calculations were made annually.

Estimates of the cost of equity for a single company are considerably less precise than estimates of the cost of equity for a portfolio of companies. The random errors that influence estimates for individual companies tend to cancel out when several firms are combined in a portfolio. Therefore we calculated the cost of equity for a given industry group by taking the simple (unweighted) average of the estimated cost of equity for the companies that make up that group.[4] By looking at the cost of equity for a group (portfolio) of companies, we minimize the influence of chance errors on our results.

To implement our approach, we thus must select a time-series of interest rates and a set of procedures for each estimation method.

Interest Rates Many factors influence bond yields. Some, such as those that influence the credit rating of a company, affect the prices of specific bonds. Others, such as anticipated inflation and government monetary policy, have an influence on the prices of all bonds. In this study we are interested only in the latter. Because the default risk on government securities is negligible, the yields on government securities provide the best indication of changes in market factors.

Debt instruments are differentiated not only by quality (default risk) but by maturity. United States government securities, for example, are available in maturities from thirteen weeks to thirty years. In addition to premiums for the risk of default and expected inflation, interest rates on long-term securities may contain maturity premiums. A maturity premium is additional compensation for holding long-term rather than short-term bonds. Differences in yields due to maturity alone do not present a problem, because we are concerned with the *change* in interest rates, not the absolute level.

The appropriate maturity for present purposes is one that corresponds to the period during which the rate decision is expected to be in effect. However, a specific period of regulatory lag usually is not defined either for particular utilities or for particular regulatory agencies. Recently, the period between hearings for most utilities has shortened to a few years at most. Since we do not know precisely which maturity is appropriate, we considered government notes of one-, three-, and five-year maturities, *INT*1, *INT*3, and *INT*5, respectively. The yields on these instruments were very similar over the period from 1971 to 1980, so the particular maturity is not important (see figure 4.1). We use the three-year note for the following work.

Estimation Methods The various estimation methods can be implemented in different ways. For the DCF approach, we constructed three estimates of the cost of equity. The baseline dividend yield was computed in the same way for each estimate; only the growth rates differ.

The dividend yield for all three DCF estimates was computed as the sum of common stock dividends during the year taken as a ratio to the year-end price for that stock. For example, the Central Maine Power Company paid common stock dividends of $1.36 in 1976. The closing price on December 31, 1976, was $16⅜. Therefore, Central Maine's dividend yield for 1976 was 8.3 percent. The expected divi-

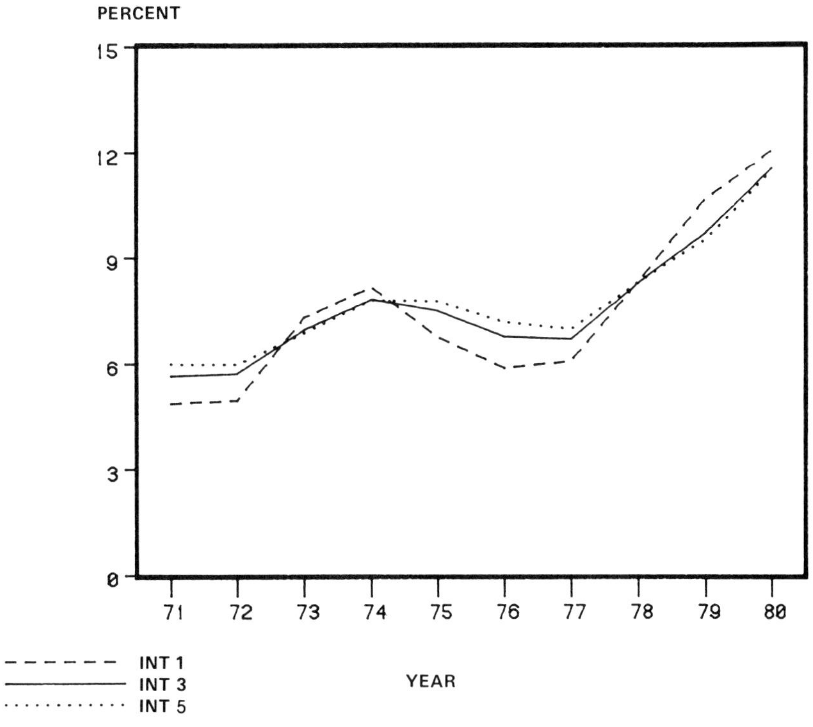

Figure 4.1
Interest Rate Comparison

dend yield equaled this baseline yield times one plus the growth rate for each DCF estimate.

The three estimates of the DCF growth rates were the ten-year trend in earnings per share, the five-year trend in earnings per share, and the "sustainable growth" rate. The ten-year trend in earnings per share, *G*1, was calculated by a least-squares regression of earnings per share on a time trend for ten years. The five-year trend, *G*2, was calculated the same way, except that only five years of data were used. The sustainable growth rate, *G*3, was calculated by multiplying the five-year average book return on equity by the earnings retention rate (the retention rate is one minus the dividend payout rate).

Three DCF estimates of the cost of capital were formed from the common baseline dividend yield and the three estimated growth rates. *DCF*1, *DCF*2 and *DCF*3 correspond to *G*1, *G*2 and *G*3.

The earnings-price ratio estimate of the cost of equity, *PE* in the figures in this chapter, was the annual earnings per share divided by the year-end stock price. For example, Central Maine Power had earnings per share of $1.75 in 1976, and the price of its common stock was $16⅜. Therefore, the earnings-price ratio for 1976 was 10.7 percent.

Two different comparable earnings estimates of the cost of equity, *ROE*, were formed. First, a set of comparable earnings estimates was formed using the industry groups in the sample itself. We used the five-year average rate of return on book equity for each unregulated[5] industry group as a comparable earnings estimate. Second, we looked at the annual book rate of return on equity for the Standard & Poor's 400 industrials.

The CAPM estimate of the cost of equity, *CAPM*, was calculated as the three-year interest rate plus the product of the estimated beta coefficient and the market-risk premium. Ibbotson and Sinquefield 1977 report an average risk premium for common stocks of 9.2 percent. We used that figure for our calculations.[6] The beta coefficient was estimated using five years of monthly data.

Possible Variations The particular procedures chosen to implement these estimation methods are not the only ones possible, nor are they necessarily the best. We only claim that they are reasonable approaches to implementing the various models and that we apply these procedures uniformly to the companies in the sample. Some discussion of possible variations on our procedures may be useful.

For the DCF method, one might select a different dividend yield or a different growth rate or both. Stock prices fluctuate and so do dividend yields. By selecting the dividend yield at a different date, or by taking an average of several dividend yields, one might obtain another value. Also, besides looking at "sustainable growth" or the growth rate of earnings per share (the procedures used here), one might use the growth rate of dividends or book equity. Another approach is to use growth rates forecast by a sample of investment advisory services.[7] For the earnings-price ratio method, a variant of the DCF, one might use annual earnings divided by some average of prices.

Analysts follow a variety of procedures for obtaining comparable earnings estimates. The general approach is to identify a group of companies that are "comparable" to the utility in question. The criteria by which comparable firms are selected are a matter of judgment;

usually they are factors the analyst believes are indicators of risk. Our work made no attempt to identify firms of any particular risk class. This is not a shortcoming, however, because we are interested in the properties of book rates of return regardless of risk. Whatever risk class a particular group of companies represents, the cost of equity should move with interest rates if comparable earnings estimates are to be useful.

The CAPM incorporates three parameters, each requiring the exercise of some judgment. In particular, one might select an interest rate for government securities with a different maturity. There are as well other approaches to estimating the beta coefficient.[8]

Results

The results of this analysis are presented in a series of graphs on which interest rates and the estimated cost of equity for each industry group are plotted. Calculations were made for all eleven industry groups, but only a representative subset of results is included.

DCF and EPR Consider first the cost of equity estimated by the DCF and the earnings-price methods (figures 4.2 to 4.6). The behavior of the estimates for the utility group is qualitatively different from those for unregulated industry groups.

For the electric utility group, the four alternative estimates of the cost of equity tend to move in tandem. They also follow the interest rate fairly well, with one important exception: in 1974, all three estimates of the cost of equity jump far more than the interest rate alone suggests they should. Of the four estimation methods, DCF2 (based on the five-year growth in earnings per share) and EPR are discernibly less accurate in tracking interest rate movements.

For the unregulated industry groups, the cost-of-equity estimates are not so well behaved. All the estimates are more volatile than those for the electric utilities. They show a greater tendency to diverge from interest rate movements. The DCF2 and EPR estimates are erratic and clearly inferior to the DCF1 and DCF3 estimates. Finally, as with the utilities, all of the estimates reacted sharply to the 1974 recession.

In general, both DCF and EPR estimates appear to be especially vulnerable to sharp reductions in stock prices. When prices drop sharply, both current dividend yield and the earnings-price ratio rise sharply; DCF growth rates estimated with historical data do not compensate for these changes. When the results for the unregulated com-

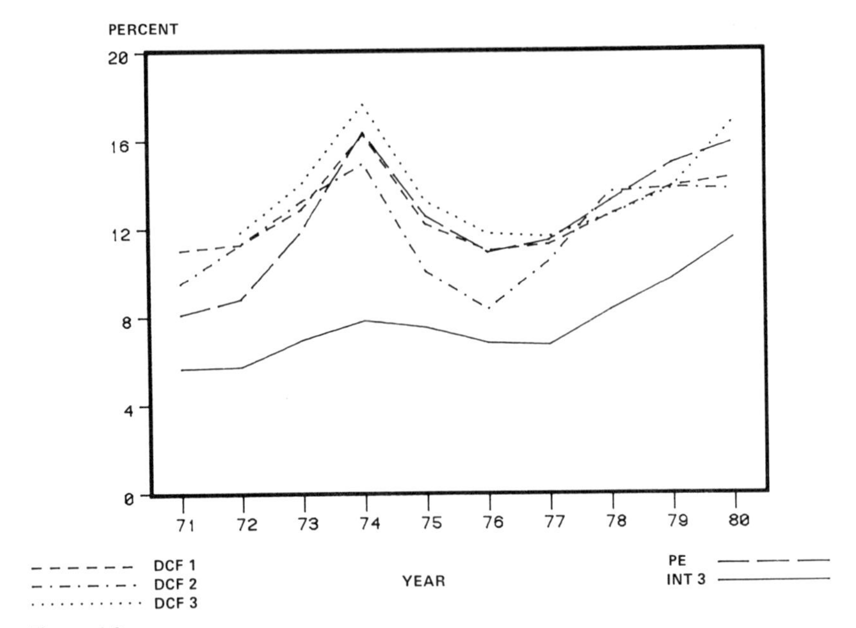

Figure 4.2
Industry Group 49: Public Utilities

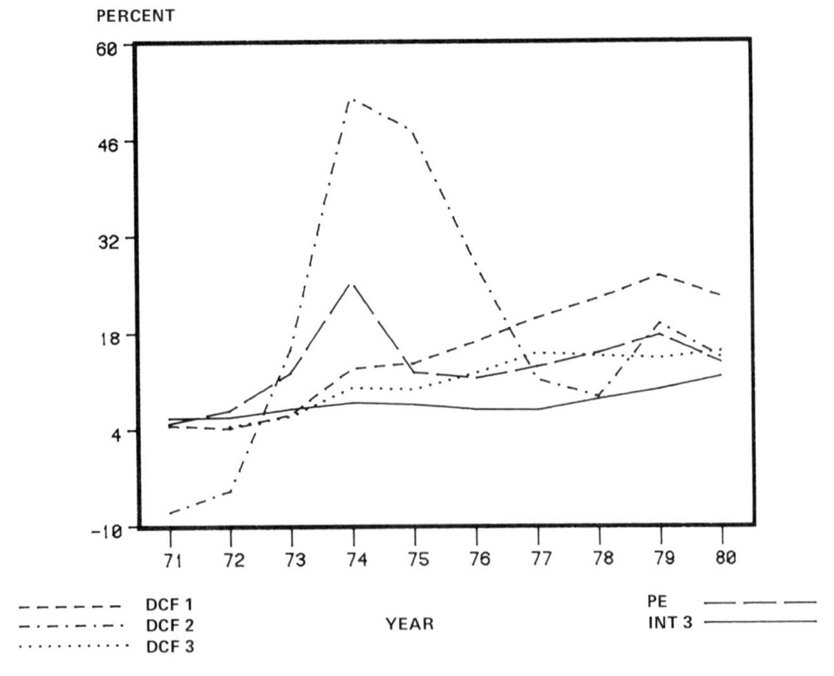

Figure 4.3
Industry Group 26: Paper and Allied Products

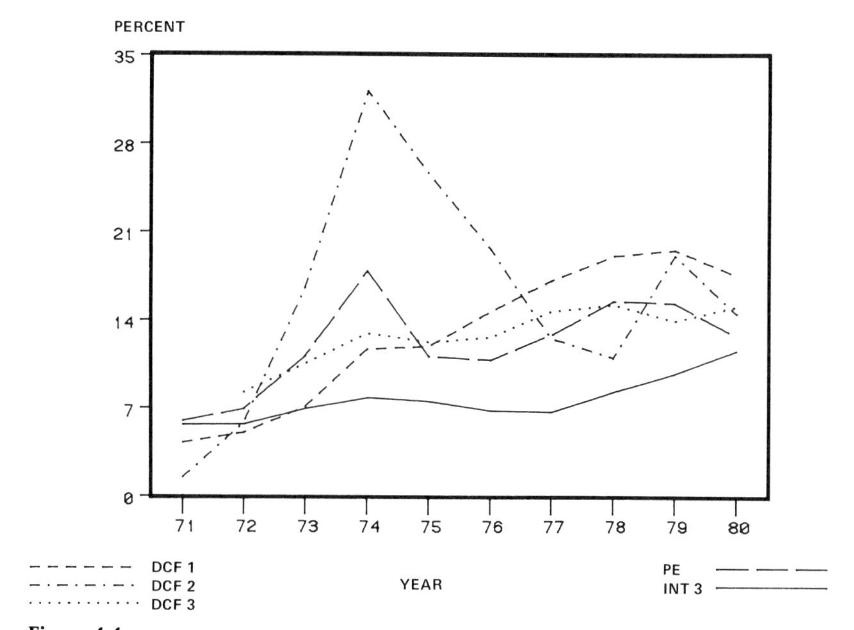

Figure 4.4
Industry Group 28: Chemicals and Allied Products

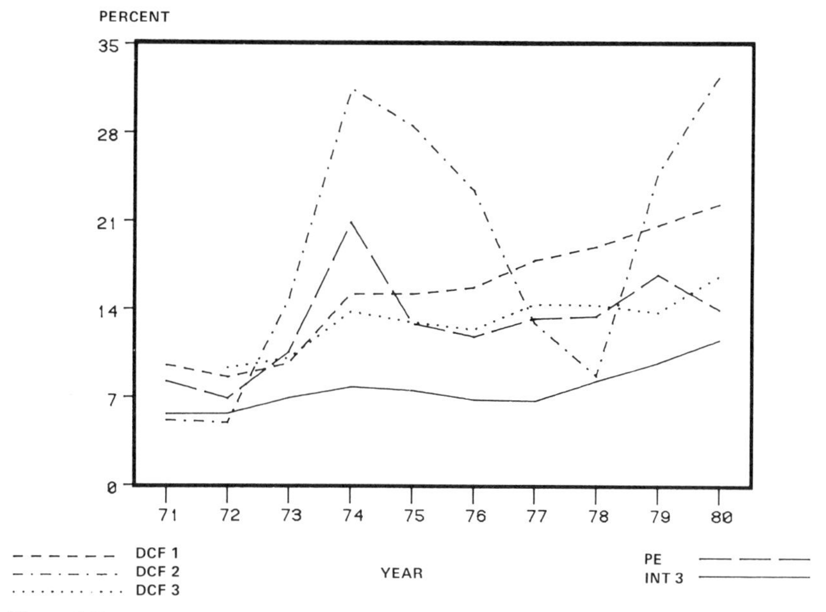

Figure 4.5
Industry Group 29: Petroleum Refining

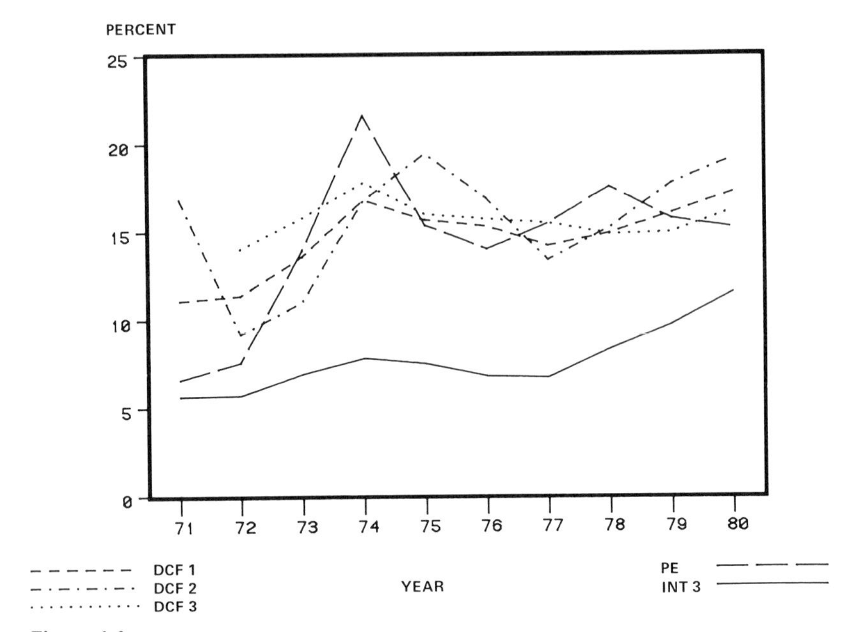

Figure 4.6
Industry Group 54: Grocery Stores

panies are considered, the DCF2 and EPR estimates are clearly inferior. DCF1 and DCF3 are roughly comparable. On the whole, the DCF3 estimate appears to be slightly better. In the following analysis, we use DCF3 to evaluate the performance of DCF relative to the CAPM and the comparable earnings test.

DCF, CE, and CAPM The cost of equity estimated by the DCF method, *DCF*3, the comparable earnings method, *ROE*, for return on equity, and the CAPM, *CAPM*, are plotted along with the three-year government interest rate, *INT*3, in figures 4.7 to 4.11.

Of the three alternatives, the CAPM clearly does the best job of tracking interest rates. This is not surprising since it incorporates the interest rate as a parameter. CAPM estimates do exhibit some deviation from interest rates due to fluctuation in the estimated beta coefficients. Nonetheless, these figures provide empirical support for the CAPM's ability to track current capital market conditions more closely than some other methods, an important advantage of CAPM, its variations, and the Risk Positioning methods discussed in chapter 3.

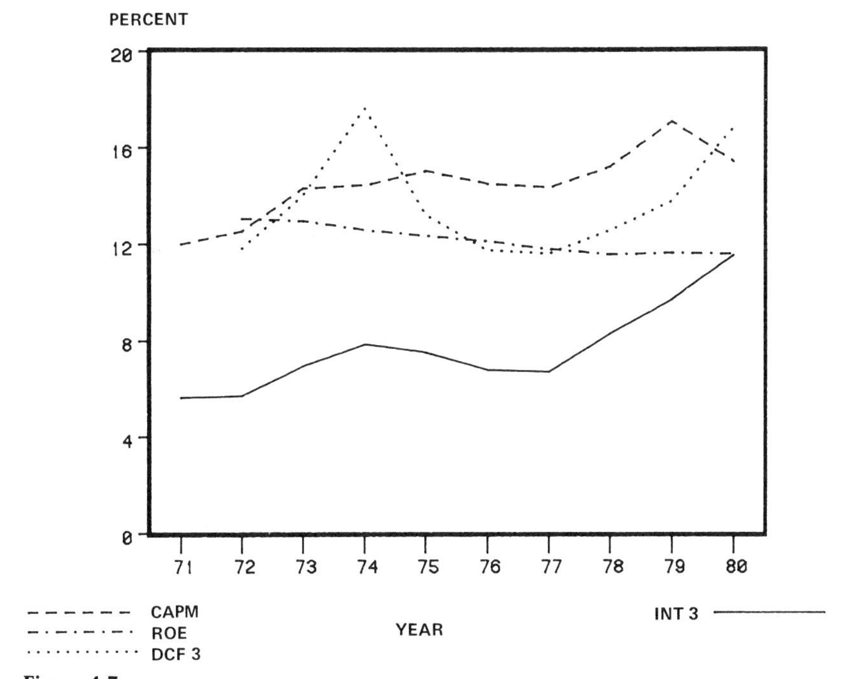

Figure 4.7
Industry Group 49: Public Utilities

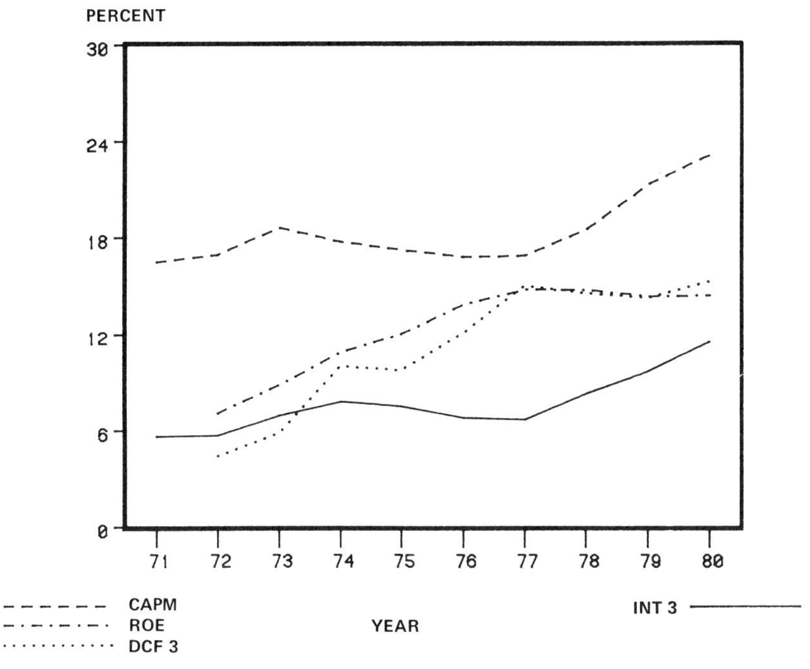

Figure 4.8
Industry Group 26: Paper and Allied Products

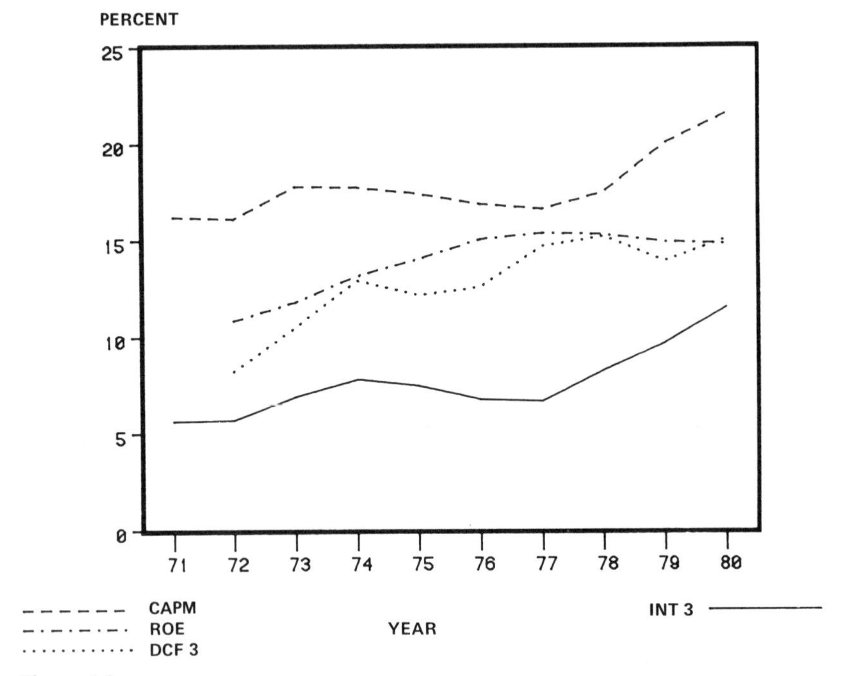

Figure 4.9
Industry Group 28: Chemicals and Allied Products

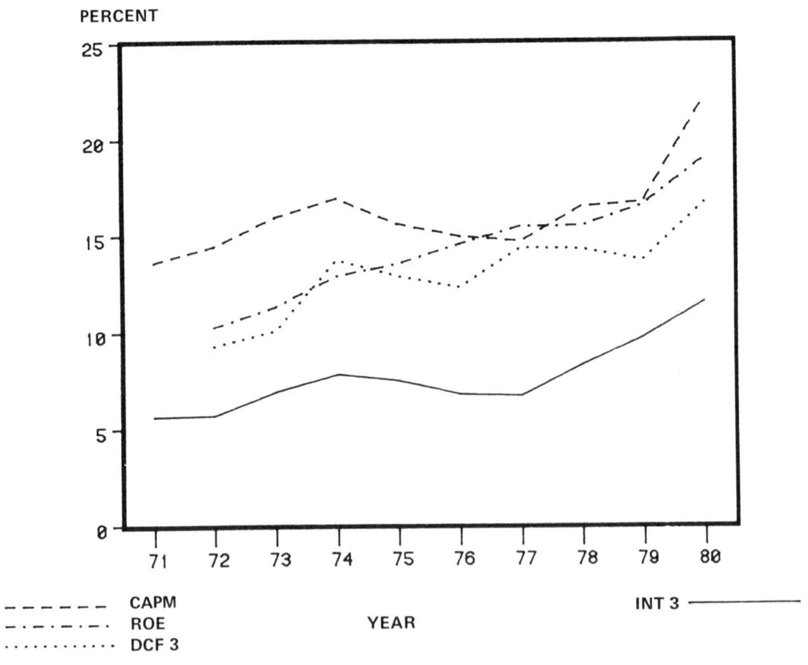

Figure 4.10
Industry Group 29: Petroleum Refining

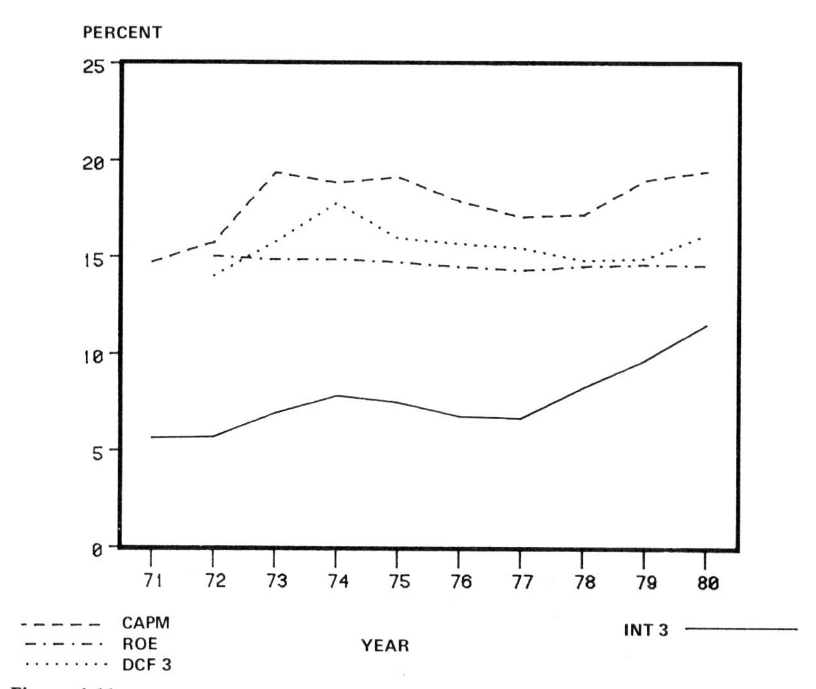

Figure 4.11
Industry Group 54: Grocery Stores

The DCF estimates tend to move with interest rates, but there is a great deal of "noise." There are many examples among the five industry groups in which the estimated cost of equity moves in the opposite direction from interest rates. Also, we continue to observe the exaggerated movement in the DCF estimates during the market decline of 1974.

The comparable earnings method scores last with respect to the interest rate test. On the whole, *ROE* tends to rise over the 1971–1980 period, as does the interest rate. But in one of the four unregulated industry groups, the *ROE* actually declines over this period. Year-to-year changes clearly do not move with interest rates.

One shortcoming of our test of the comparable earnings method is that we used the five-year average return on equity. This was done because we know that the business cycle affects the book return on equity. While the average smooths out the business cycle, it may also smooth changes in *ROE* due to relevant factors. As an alternative, we looked at an annual return on equity. Figure 4.12 displays the

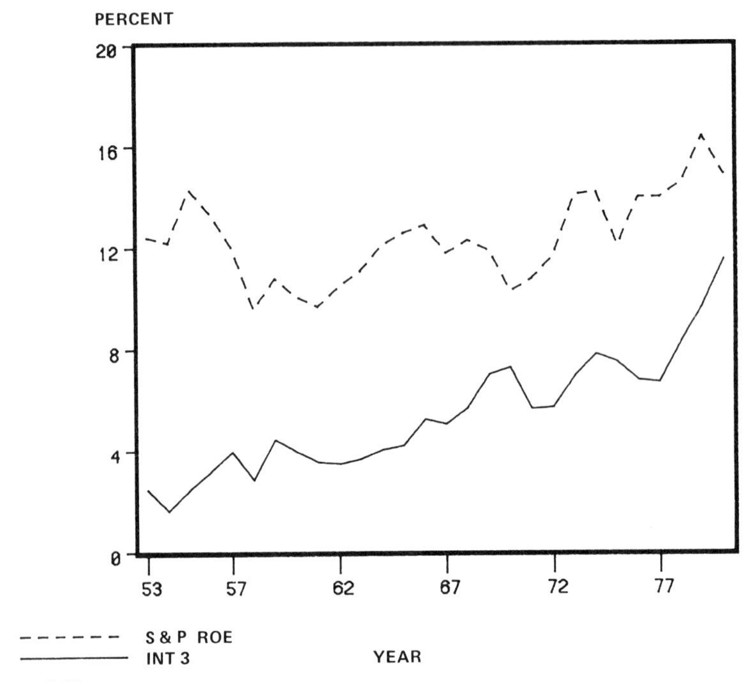

Figure 4.12
Standard and Poor's Industrials: Return on Equity

book return on equity for the Standard & Poor's index of industrial companies.

A first look suggests that the *ROE* does move with interest rates. But look more closely. While there are periods, such as 1957 to 1962, when the *ROE* moves with interest rates, there are other periods in which changes in *ROE* contradict changes in interest rates. The most striking example is 1953 to 1957, in which the implied risk premium goes from about 10 percent to 6 percent. Another period in which the book *ROE* and interest rates moved in opposite directions is 1968 to 1972. Thus the historical data suggest that *ROE* poorly reflects changes in the capital markets.

Summary With respect to our first test—the ability to track changes in interest rates—the CAPM is the best of the three methods, followed by the DCF method in a distant second place, and comparable earnings pulling up the rear. A few points are worth special note.

First, the CAPM includes the interest rate as a parameter. It is not surprising therefore that it performs better than the alternatives with respect to this criterion. (This is one of the advantages of the CAPM and other risk-positioning methods.) Second, the DCF estimates follow interest rates considerably better for the electric utilities than for unregulated firms—a reminder that this approach works best in an environment of stable earnings and prices. Third, the earnings-price ratio estimates are particularly volatile for the unregulated companies. They respond more sharply to business cycle troughs than the alternative DCF estimates. Finally, comparable earnings estimates appear to respond to many factors other than capital market conditions, especially the business cycle. This method therefore provides spurious signals about capital costs.

With respect to comparisons among the methods, the alternative DCF estimates for the electric utility group—including the earnings-price ratio—moved together. However, the DCF method generated a wide range of estimates of the unregulated industry groups. In particular, the DCF estimates derived from the five-year trend in earnings per share and the earnings-price ratio were erratic when applied to the unregulated industry groups.

Finally, the CAPM estimates of the cost of equity are consistently higher than the DCF and comparable earnings estimates. This is probably due to the particular sample period, over which capital costs generally were rising, rather than to any inherent tendency for the CAPM to yield higher estimates than the alternatives. (For example, with rising capital costs, historical data will tend to underpredict the DCF growth rate that investors currently expect.)

The Stability of Key Parameters

Several components are embodied in an equation relating the cost of equity to one or more financial parameters. For example, the CAPM specifies the cost of equity in terms of an interest rate, a beta coefficient, and the market-risk premium. Similarly, the DCF model contains a dividend yield and growth rate. These parameters—or more precisely estimates of these parameters—fluctuate from period to period. We will focus on the stability of two parameters in particular: the beta coefficient and the DCF growth rate.

A series of bar graphs illustrates the stability of the estimated beta coefficient during the period from 1971 to 1980 (figures 4.13 to 4.15). These are drawn for the electric utility industry group and for two

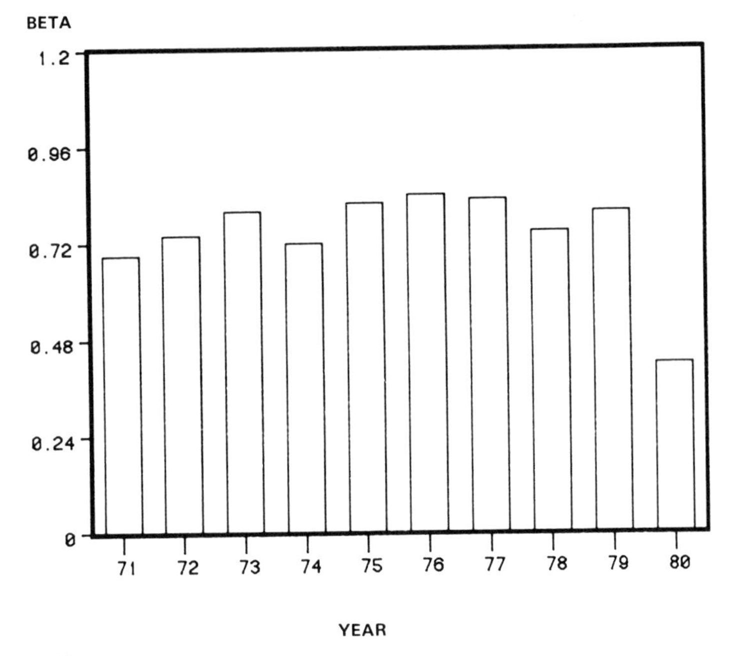

Figure 4.13
Electrical Utilities: BETA

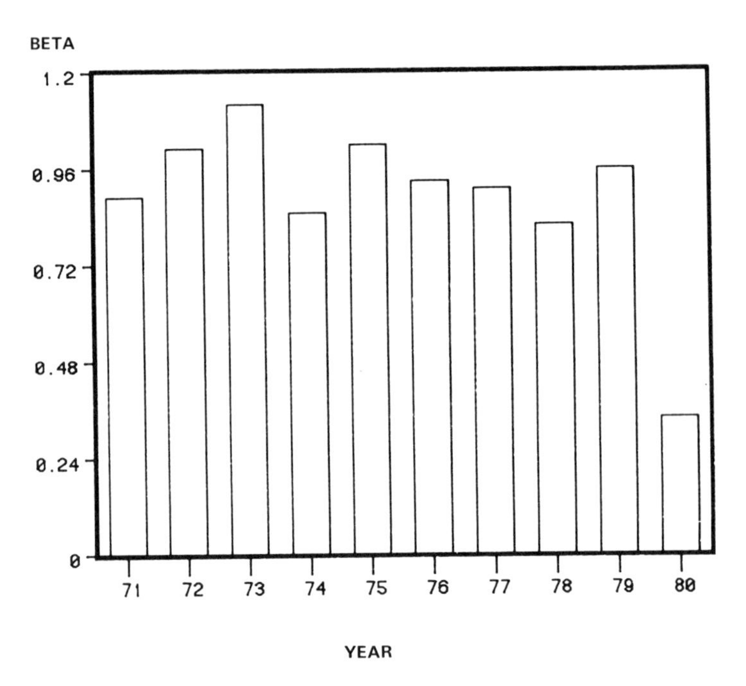

Figure 4.14
Florida Power and Light: BETA

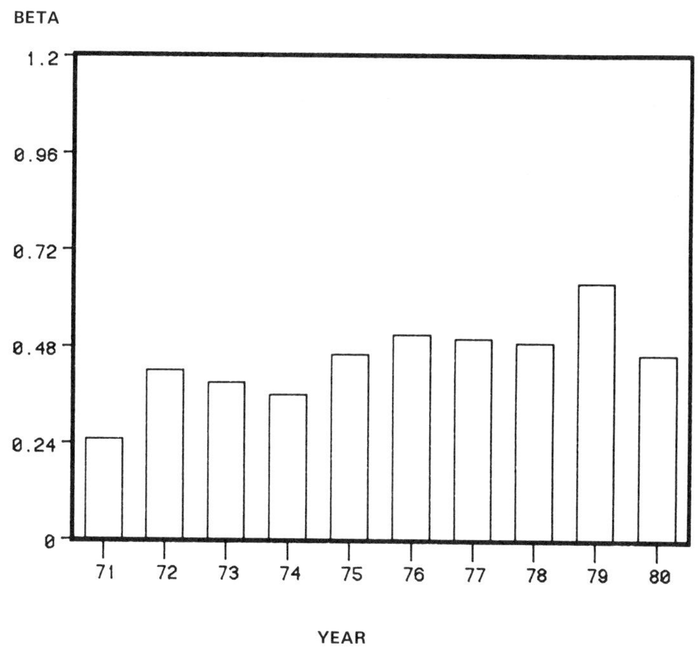

Figure 4.15
Central Maine Power: BETA

particular utilities. Over this period the beta coefficient for the utilities group ranged from about 0.42 to 0.84. If the 1980 period is neglected, the range is 0.69 to 0.84. For the group as a whole beta was quite stable. The estimated beta for Florida Power & Light ranged from 0.34 to 1.12. If 1980 is neglected, the range is 0.82 to 1.12. For Central Maine Power beta ranged from 0.25 to 0.64. Individual stock betas showed considerably more fluctuation than the group beta. This is as expected, however, since random errors tend to cancel out in portfolios of stocks.

The utility stock betas for 1980 are clearly outliers. When we first discovered this result, we surmised the following. Utility stocks have many of the characteristics of a bond (for this reason they are sometimes referred to as "pseudoequities"). Bond returns appeared to become more volatile in 1980, perhaps because of the Federal Reserve Board's actions following its much-publicized October 1979 switch in emphasis to monetary growth targets. Also, because the stock market showed a large gain at the same time the bond market went through a substantial decline, 1980 was an unusual year. The negative correlation between stocks and bonds in 1980 may be a source of the anomalous beta estimate.

Our surmise is that the "missing asset" criticism of the CAPM was especially important for electric utilities in 1980. Utility betas with respect to a value-weighted stock and bond "market portfolio" would be higher. Since preparing these graphs we have had the opportunity to test our surmise. We found that when bonds as well as stocks are included in the market index used to calculate betas, and when the results are adjusted to make them comparable to traditional betas, utility betas are consistently higher even back as far as the 1960s and do not show dramatic declines in 1980 or 1981. Similar results were obtained for gas utilities and operating telephone companies but not for unregulated industries: unregulated betas show no consistent pattern over time and are generally insensitive to the definition of the market.[9] We do not wish to make too much of this particular study, but it does indicate a problem with conventional estimates of utility betas that we have not seen described or documented elsewhere.

Bar graphs were also used to illustrate the stability of estimated DCF growth rates. (Since growth rates estimated by the five-year trend in earnings per share, *G*2, were erratic, they are neglected here.) Figures 4.16 to 4.18 show the range of values obtained for *G*1, the ten-year trend in earnings per share. It ranged from 1.8 percent to 5.4 percent for the utilities group; from 1.3 to 3.6 for Central Maine Power; and from 6.0 to 9.5 for Florida Power & Light. Figures 4.19 to 4.21 show the range of values obtained for *G*3, the sustainable growth rate. It varied from 2.3 to 6.0 percent for the utilities group; from 5.8 to 10.6 percent for Florida Power & Light; and from 0.6 to 3.0 percent for Central Maine Power.

These figures suggest that unlike betas, growth rates for the group of utilities were not a great deal more stable than for individual utilities using these estimation methods. The sustainable growth rate is more stable than the trend in earnings per share.

We also conducted an alternative test of parameter stability. The eleven industry groups were ranked according to a given parameter in one year. The groups were then ranked again using parameter values obtained for a subsequent year and the two rankings were compared. The more stable the parameter, the more stable we expect the industry rankings to be.

The two years, 1972 and 1978, were selected arbitrarily. As a guide to stability we counted the number of groups that changed more than

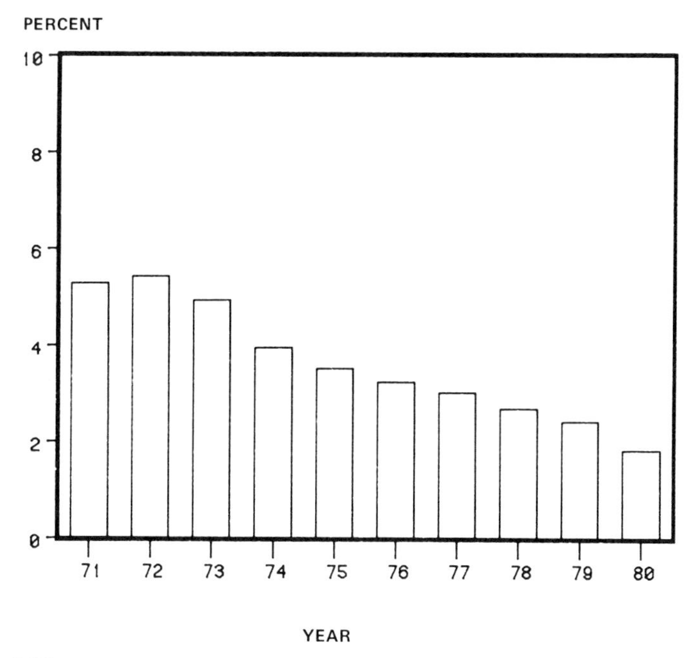

Figure 4.16
Electric Utilities: G1

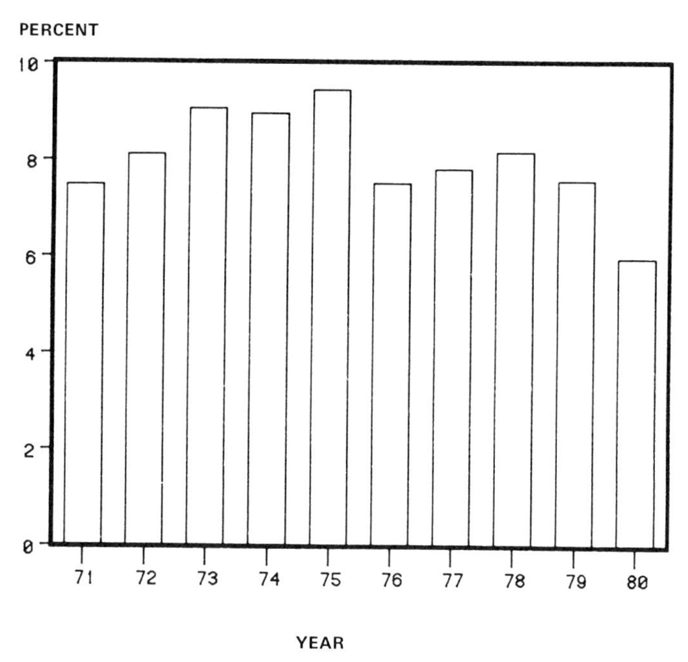

Figure 4.17
Florida Power and Light: G1

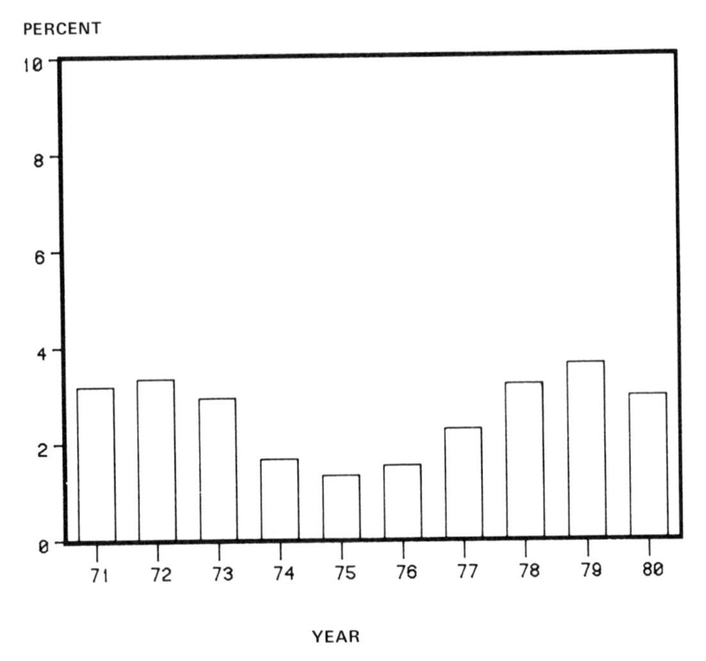

Figure 4.18
Central Maine Power: G1

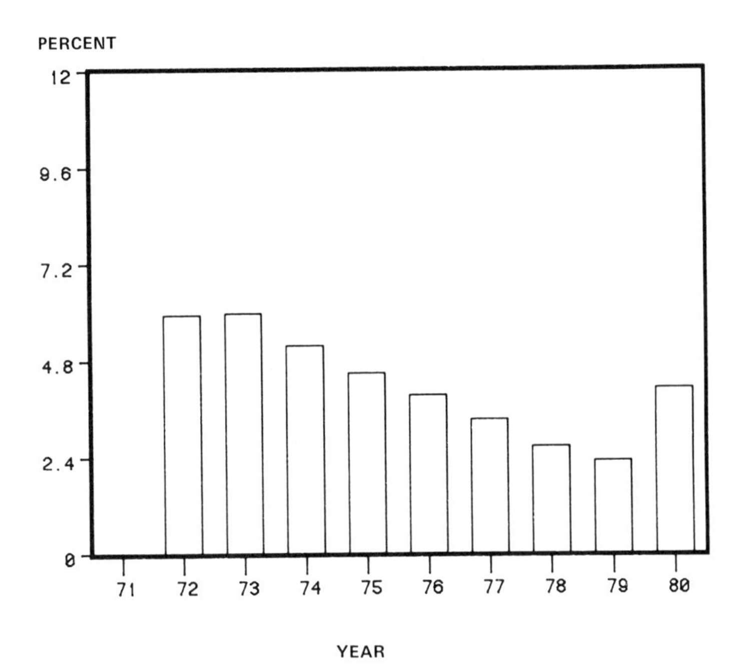

Figure 4.19
Electric Utilities: G3

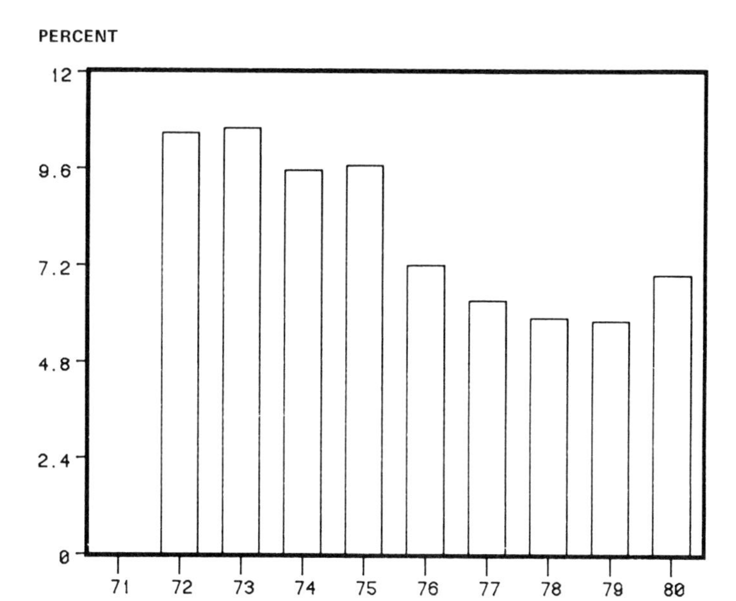

Figure 4.20
Florida Power and Light: G3

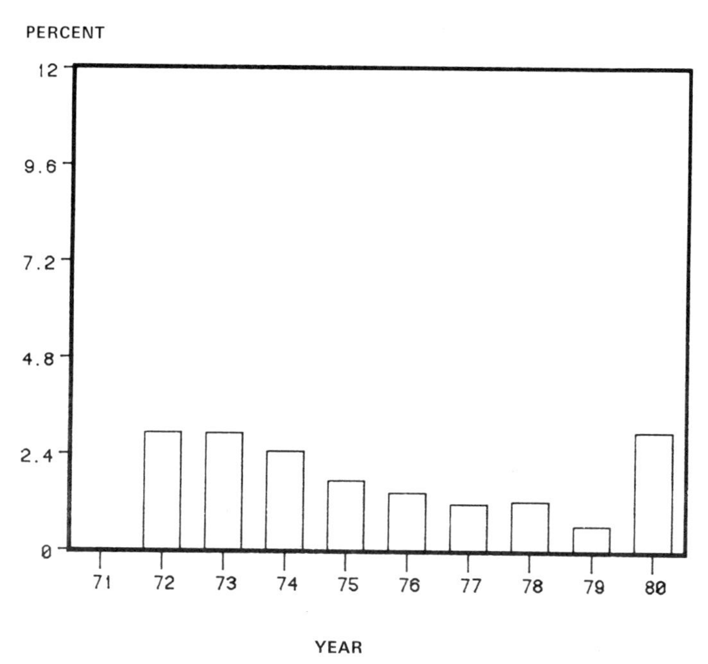

Figure 4.21
Central Maine Power: G3

Table 4.1
Return on equity (five-year average)

Industry group	1972 value	1978 value	1972 rank	1978 rank
Food	14.27	16.54	2	1
Textiles	8.16	11.71	8	9
Paper	7.11	14.76	10	5[a]
Chemicals	10.86	15.31	6	4
Petroleum	10.29	15.48	7	3[a]
Steel	6.73	13.80	11	7[a]
Motor vehicle parts	13.03	15.87	4	2
Railroads	8.04	9.11	9	11
Electric utilities	13.04	11.57	3	10[a]
Department stores	11.23	11.94	5	8[a]
Grocery stores	15.04	14.56	1	6[a]

a. Indicates a change in rank of more than two places.

two places from 1972 to 1978. The results are reported in tables 4.1 to 4.3. We looked at the (five-year average) return on equity, the beta coefficient, and the ten-year trend in earnings per share.

According to this test, the beta coefficient was the most stable of the three parameters we examined, the return on equity the next most stable, and the DCF growth rate was the least stable. Two industry groups had a large change in ranking according to beta, six groups according to the return on equity, and eight groups according to the DCF growth rate.

Robustness of Alternative Methods

Each method of estimating the cost of equity requires the analyst to exercise a certain amount of judgment. The comparable earnings method requires that the analyst select a sample of comparable firms. The DCF model requires the analyst select a value for the long-term growth rate. The CAPM requires an estimate of the beta coefficient. All these demand judgment. What criteria are used to identify "comparable" firms? How should the long-term growth rate be estimated? What value is to be used for the beta coefficient? We make no attempt to provide answers to these questions; our objective is to examine the

Table 4.2
Beta coefficient

Industry group	1972 value	1978 value	1972 rank	1978 rank
Food	0.83	0.86	10	9
Textiles	1.16	0.96	5	6
Paper	1.22	1.11	3	1
Chemicals	1.13	1.00	6	3[a]
Petroleum	0.95	0.89	9	8
Steel	1.07	0.76	8	10
Motor vehicle parts	1.22	0.98	4	4
Railroads	1.30	0.96	2	7[a]
Electric utilities	0.74	0.75	11	11
Department stores	1.31	1.06	1	2
Grocery stores	1.09	0.97	7	5

a. Indicates a change in rank of more than two places.

Table 4.3
Growth rate (ten-year trend in earnings)

Industry group	1972 value	1978 value	1972 rank	1978 rank
Food	7.47	12.68	2	4
Textiles	−0.31	10.33	10	7[a]
Paper	0.46	16.65	9	1[a]
Chemicals	1.70	12.40	8	5[a]
Petroleum	4.31	12.80	5	3
Steel	−3.73	16.61	11	2[a]
Motor vehicle parts	3.00	10.37	7	6
Railroads	3.27	7.50	6	10[a]
Electric utilities	5.43	2.70	4	11[a]
Department stores	6.78	9.23	3	8[a]
Grocery stores	7.59	8.85	1	9[a]

a. Indicates a change in rank of more than two places.

sensitivity of the estimated cost of equity to changes in the way the methodologies are implemented.

Qualitative analysis of the DCF model and the CAPM can provide a rough guide to the robustness of these two approaches. Specifically, the growth rate enters the DCF estimate of the cost of equity directly. Alternative growth rates differing by, for example, three percentage points (not an improbable finding based on the data reported in this chapter), imply a difference in the cost of equity of (somewhat more than[10]) three percentage points. In the CAPM, the utility-risk premium is equal to the product of the beta coefficient and the market-risk premium. If we use the market-risk premium estimated by Ibbotson and Sinquefield (approximately 9 percent), alternative beta estimates differing by, say, 0.1 to 0.2 (again not improbable for an industry, *providing* that the "missing asset" problem is avoided) imply a difference in the cost of equity of roughly one to two percentage points. Thus if industry-wide betas are used, CAPM estimates seem likely to be less sensitive to variations in the key unknown parameter than DCF estimates.[11]

Using data from our sample of companies and elsewhere, we made a quantitative assessment of the robustness of several methods, including the comparable earnings approach and the DCF model. Figures 4.2 to 4.6 suggest the range of estimates obtainable with alternative applications of the DCF approach. For the electric utility group, the range was as little as 1.0 percent (1978) and as large as 3.4 percent (1976).

Recent testimony submitted in the state of Alabama examined several alternative methods of estimating the DCF growth rate (table 4.4). These included sustainable growth; growth in earnings per share, dividends, and book equity; and the forecast of a major investment advisory service. Data were compiled for six different utilities. The range of growth rates obtained using these different approaches was as narrow as 3.1 percent for one utility and as wide as 10.9 percent for another.

Turning to the comparable earnings method, the average return on equity for each of the ten unregulated industry groups can be taken as a comparable earnings estimate of the cost of equity. Of course, a witness would select a set of comparable firms on the basis of one or more risk factors. It is unlikely that each of the industry groups would fall into the same risk category, however defined.

To allow for risk differences, we note that the beta coefficient is one

Table 4.4
Alternative growth rate estimates

	ATT	Cincinnati Bell	Mid-Continent Telephone	Pacific Telephone Telegraph	Rochester Telephone	Southern New England Telephone	Average
Sustainable growth[a]	5.07	7.82	7.20	2.91	6.54	4.14	5.62
Common equity[b]	9.95	10.67	14.22	2.62	9.96	7.56	9.16
Earnings per share[b]	10.02	9.02	8.54	0.00	17.42	8.47	8.91
Dividends per share[b]	8.02	9.51	9.78	3.13	17.44	5.25	8.86
Value line estimate	7.50	6.50	6.50	2.50	9.00	7.50	6.58
Range	4.95	4.17	7.72	3.13	10.90	4.33	3.54

a. Five-year average sustainable growth, 1975–1980.
b. Compound growth rate, 1975–1980.
Source: Testimony of Robert B. Morris III for Continental Telephone of the South, Alabama.

objective measure of risk. (According to the CAPM it is *the* relevant measure of risk.) Using the beta coefficient, it is possible to identify several industry groups within our sample that are in the same risk class (table 4.5). In 1972 industry groups 33, 28, and 54 all had beta values of approximately 1.1. Yet group 33 had a five-year average *ROE* of 6.7 percent, group 28 had an *ROE* of 10.9 percent, and group 54 had an *ROE* of 15.0 percent. Therefore, one reasonable implementation of comparable earnings yields a range of 8.3 percent in the cost of equity. The same approach can be taken with 1978. Five industry groups have beta values of 1.0. The five-year average *ROE* for these five ranges from 9.1 percent for group 40 to 16.5 percent for group 20.

A more important result demonstrated by table 4.5 is the apparent absence of a relationship between book rates of return and risk. This is true for both years examined. In fact, the sample correlation coefficient for 1972 and 1978 are −0.15 and −0.37, respectively. This means that in the samples used for this study, there was actually an inverse relationship between risk and book rate of return. This is evidence that the accounting (book) rate of return and the economic rate of return are two different things and that the relationship between them is tenuous at best.

Conclusions on Inferred Accuracy

Several points from the above analyses should be stressed. The cost of equity estimates for the electric utility industry group were more stable than the corresponding estimates for unregulated industry groups. In part this is a reflection of the relative stability of electric utility earnings. However, it also reflects the important point that estimates for portfolios of companies are more precise than estimates for individual stocks. (Part of the apparent stability of cost-of-equity estimates for utilities comes from the fact that our utility industry group included more companies than the other industry groups; see appendix C.)

Turning to the relative merits of the methods themselves, the DCF method did a reasonably good job of following changes in interest rates. An important exception, especially for the electric utilities, was 1974. When stock prices move sharply, DCF estimates appear to be exaggerated. On the other criteria, the DCF method did not score as well. The growth rate parameter was quite unstable, at least for the methods by which we estimated it. Furthermore, there are many

Table 4.5
Robustness of comparable earnings

A. 1972

Industry group	*ROE*[a]	Beta	*ROE* rank	Beta rank[b]
33: Steel	6.7	1.07	10	8
26: Paper	7.1	1.22	9	4
40: Railroads	8.0	1.30	8	2
22: Textiles	8.2	1.16	7	5
29: Petroleum	10.3	0.95	6	9
28: Chemicals	10.9	1.13	5	6
53: Department stores	11.2	1.31	4	1
37: Motor vehicle parts	13.0	1.22	3	3
20: Food	14.3	0.83	2	10
54: Grocery stores	15.0	1.09	1	7

B. 1978

Industry group	*ROE*[a]	Beta	*ROE* rank	Beta rank[c]
40: Railroads	9.1	0.96	10	6
22: Textiles	11.7	0.96	9	7
53: Department stores	11.9	1.06	8	2
33: Steel	13.8	0.76	7	10
54: Grocery stores	14.6	0.97	6	5
26: Paper	14.8	1.11	5	1
28: Chemicals	15.3	1.00	4	3
29: Petroleum	15.5	0.89	3	8
37: Motor vehicle parts	15.9	0.98	2	4
20: Food	16.5	0.86	1	9

a. Five-year average returns on equity.
b. Sample correlation coefficient between *ROE* and beta is −0.15.
c. Sample correlation coefficient between *ROE* and beta is −0.37.

possible methods for estimating growth rates, and the range of resulting estimates indicates that the DCF method is not very robust to minor changes in application.

The CAPM followed changes in interest rates very well. While this is not surprising, since it incorporates the interest rate as a parameter, it does confirm the advantage of risk-positioning approaches in tracking current capital market conditions. The beta parameter turned out to be relatively stable, particularly when we considered the beta for industry groups.

Finally, the comparable earnings test scored poorly with respect to its ability to track changes in interest rates. The average return on equity for a group of companies is also rather unstable, even when used to rank industry groups. Moreover, alternative applications of the comparable earnings test can produce a wide range of results, so this method scores poorly on the robustness criterion.

Acceptability of Alternative Methods to Regulators

Our last evaluative criterion is regulatory use. Ideally, it would be desirable to examine a large sample of commission decisions and collect direct evidence concerning the methods on which commissions actually rely. However, commissions rarely cite a specific witness or technique as the source of their allowed rate of return; they seem to prefer to rely on "the weight of the evidence" instead. Thus we must turn to another source of information.

The National Association of Regulatory Utility Commissioners (NARUC) publishes an *Annual Report on Utility and Carrier Regulation.* Included in each report is a summary of the methods favored by each regulatory agency for determining the allowed rate of return. In addition to the fifty states and the District of Columbia, this summary includes four provinces of Canada, three United States possessions, the FCC, and the FERC.

The report is self-explanatory and easily obtained; we will only summarize some of its contents, to complete our evaluation and to indicate the kind of information available.

According to the 1980 report approximately one half of the regulatory agencies indicated a clear preference for either one or two methods. The comparable earnings and discounted cash flow methods are most often cited by these agencies.

Twenty-one agencies cited a single preferred method. Of these, nine favored discounted cash flow, five favored comparable earnings, one favored the capital asset pricing model, one the earnings-price ratio method, and five did not specify which method was preferred.

Twelve agencies cited two preferred approaches. In this category, the comparable earnings method was cited most often, eleven times. DCF was cited six times, the price-earnings ratio method three times, the market-to-book ratio once, the CAPM once, and two indicated an unspecified method.

Some changes had occurred by the 1981 report. Thirty-five agencies indicated one or more specific methods. Comparable earnings and discounted cash flow were again the most often cited.

Nineteen agencies preferred a particular method. Discounted cash flow was cited eleven times, comparable earnings four times, and the capital asset pricing model once. Three did not indicate which method was preferred.

Eleven agencies indicated two separate methods, citing discounted cash flow nine times, comparable earnings eight times, earnings-price ratio twice, and the market-to-book ratio, capital asset pricing model, and "midpoint" method once each.[12]

From this and other, more casual evidence, we have the impression that regulators are in the process of turning away from the comparable earnings approach and are usually adopting the DCF method in its place. The CAPM and other methods are still also-rans. But the same could once have been said about DCF. Initially, DCF often was viewed as an exotic methodology promulgated by ivory-tower academics, just as the CAPM seems to be viewed today.

Our conclusions are that changes in the methods regulators use do occur if the superiority of a new method is sufficiently convincing but that such changes are slow. Given this apparent inertia, those writing or evaluating rate-of-return testimony will need to be familiar with a variety of methods for some time to come.

2. Summary of the Relative Merits of the Five Major Methods

We have demonstrated that no single method is best according to every criterion. Some do well on the theoretical criteria and poorly on the practical criteria. This not unexpected result leads to one important conclusion: choice of a method depends heavily on the relative importance of the different criteria to the person doing the choosing. It also depends on the state of financial markets; problems with one or another method that can be swept under the rug in quiet times may cause serious biases when financial markets are in flux unless corrective actions are taken. The relative importance attached to the different criteria is a topic on which reasonable people can disagree quite sharply.

Given the diversity of opinion and the variations often found in the estimates themselves, it is natural to ask whether the exercise is worth the effort. To answer, one must first identify an alternative. That is, if a formal attempt to estimate the cost of capital is not made, what procedure could be used instead to set the allowed rate of return? We find no good answer to this question. "Judgment" ties the rate of return to no standard and "tradition" could leave a return on equity at an absurd rate for years, perhaps one derived when interest rates were 3 percent.

We know that failing to equate the allowed rate of return with the cost of capital has high costs. We know how difficult it is to estimate the cost of capital precisely. Nonetheless, the formal process of applying a method and analyzing its likely biases under current conditions should enable a careful analyst to identify the right neighborhood for the current cost of capital. Deciding on the exact "address" within that neighborhood remains a difficult and controversial task. In our view, reliance on formal cost-of-capital estimation procedures is likely to lead to far more accurate answers than any alternauve of which we can conceive, especially in volatile times.

Turning to the summary comparison of the methods, we note that assigning a numerical score to how well a method satisfies a particular criterion would be very difficult and probably misleading; the relative rankings are simply not clear enough. Instead, we use three scores: + indicates better than average, 0 indicates about average, and − indicates below average. If the exact score depends in part on exactly how the method is applied (for example, how complicated the risk premium calculation is in the Risk Positioning approach), a "?" is used.

We have explained the reasons for our choices in detail. Others might well give different scores; some subjectivity is unavoidable in such a procedure. With this caveat, table 4.6 gives our scores.

No method is completely dominated by the others, although Comparable Earnings comes very close (it is saved only by its long history of regulatory use, a somewhat questionable advantage given its other problems). Some methods are less sensitive than others to the inevita-

Table 4.6
Evaluation summary

Criterion	Method				
	Comparable Earnings	Discounted Cash Flow	Capital Asset Pricing Model	Risk Positioning	Market-to-Book Ratio
1. Logical consistency	+/−	+	+	+	−
2. Consistency with theory	−	0	+	+	+/−
3. Data requirements	0	+	0	?	+
4. Related costs	+	+	−	?	+
5. Inferred accuracy	−	0	+	+	a
6. Regulatory use	+	+	0	0	0

Note:
+ = above average/good
0 = average/acceptable
− = below average/poor
? = ambiguity; depends on exact details of method
If a method gets more than one score (e.g., comparable earnings on logical consistency), the implication is that there are two theories or assumptions involved and each scores differently.
a. Not tested.

ble differences between theory and application (the Capital Asset Pricing Model and Risk Positioning), and so deserve more weight in reaching a decision than routine applications of more sensitive methods. Nonetheless, all methods are potentially helpful, *providing* that the witness and the commission are sensitive to the kinds of biases that may be present and make serious attempts to correct for these biases (admittedly a far harder task for very sensitive methods, such as Comparable Earnings) in arriving at a rate of return.

5 A Look Ahead: New Approaches to Cost-of-Capital Estimation

To this point, we have concentrated on methods in wide use. This chapter focuses on methods used rarely or not at all, but which should not be overlooked. Specifically, we will consider three new methods: the "empirical" Capital Asset Pricing Model advocated by Litzenberger, Ramaswamy and Sosin (LRS) 1980; an approach developed by Pogue 1979a for use when no market data are available; and approaches equivalent to "multifactor" versions of the Capital Asset Pricing Model.

1. The "Empirical" Capital Asset Pricing Model

The "empirical" Capital Asset Pricing Model (ECAPM) has been used in a few rate hearings.[1] As developed by LRS 1980 it is an attempt to find a practical answer to the criticisms of the CAPM. We believe it is one reasonable approach to dealing with the criticisms of the CAPM, and if its parameters prove sufficiently stable it may become a useful approach in the future.

Definition and Assumptions

The rationale for the ECAPM is summarized in the discussion of the criticisms of the CAPM. The basic idea is to bypass the need for sophisticated theoretical extensions of the CAPM. The ECAPM uses data on the actual behavior of the market to obtain estimates of the cost of capital from an equation representing an approximation to the more complicated theoretical models.

The basic ECAPM equation is an extension of equation (3.11), the equation of the "pure" CAPM. For convenience, the CAPM equation is reproduced here as

$$E(r_j) = r_f + \{\beta_j \times [E(r_m) - r_f]\} \tag{5.1}$$

which translates as

$$\begin{array}{c} \text{Expected} \\ \text{rate of re-} \\ \text{turn for} \\ \text{asset } j \end{array} = \begin{array}{c} \text{Current} \\ \text{risk-free} \\ \text{rate of} \\ \text{return} \end{array} + \left[\begin{array}{c} \text{Asset's} \\ \text{beta} \end{array} \times \left(\begin{array}{c} \text{Expected} \\ \text{rate of} \\ \text{return} \\ \text{for the} \\ \text{market} \end{array} - \begin{array}{c} \text{Current} \\ \text{risk-free} \\ \text{rate of} \\ \text{return} \end{array} \right) \right].$$

The ECAPM equation is[2]

$$E(r_j) = r_f + a + (\beta_j \times b), \tag{5.2}$$

which translates as

$$\begin{array}{c} \text{Expected} \\ \text{rate of re-} \\ \text{turn for} \\ \text{asset } j \end{array} = \begin{array}{c} \text{Current} \\ \text{risk-free} \\ \text{rate of} \\ \text{return} \end{array} + \begin{array}{c} \text{A market-} \\ \text{wide con-} \\ \text{stant es-} \\ \text{timated} \\ \text{statistically} \end{array} + \left(\begin{array}{c} \text{Asset's} \\ \text{beta} \end{array} \times \begin{array}{c} \text{Another} \\ \text{market-wide} \\ \text{constant} \\ \text{estimated} \\ \text{statistically} \end{array} \right).$$

The ECAPM equation, (5.2), adds a constant, a, to all required rates of return and makes the impact of beta proportional to another constant, b, instead of to the market-risk premium. This equation approximately corrects for some of the theoretical and empirical problems researchers believe exist for the pure CAPM, at least when it is applied only to assets traded on the New York Stock Exchange.

Figure 5.1 depicts an application of the ECAPM. Figure 5.1 starts from figure 3.2, the CAPM graph in chapter 3. The CAPM line is the heavy sloped line; the ECAPM line is the lighter sloped line. Several points should be noted. First, both the ECAPM and the CAPM lines pass through the same point in the middle of the graph, where beta equals one and the expected rate of return equals $E(r_m)$. However, the ECAPM line is flatter: it intersects the vertical axis at a rate of return equal to $(r_f + a)$, higher than the CAPM intersection at r_f. The ECAPM predicts higher required rates of return than the CAPM for low-beta stocks and lower rates of return for high-beta stocks (see figure 5.1).

LRS statistically estimate the constants, a and b, using an econometric approach that is somewhat more complicated than ordinary least-squares regressions, because of the nature of the data.[3]

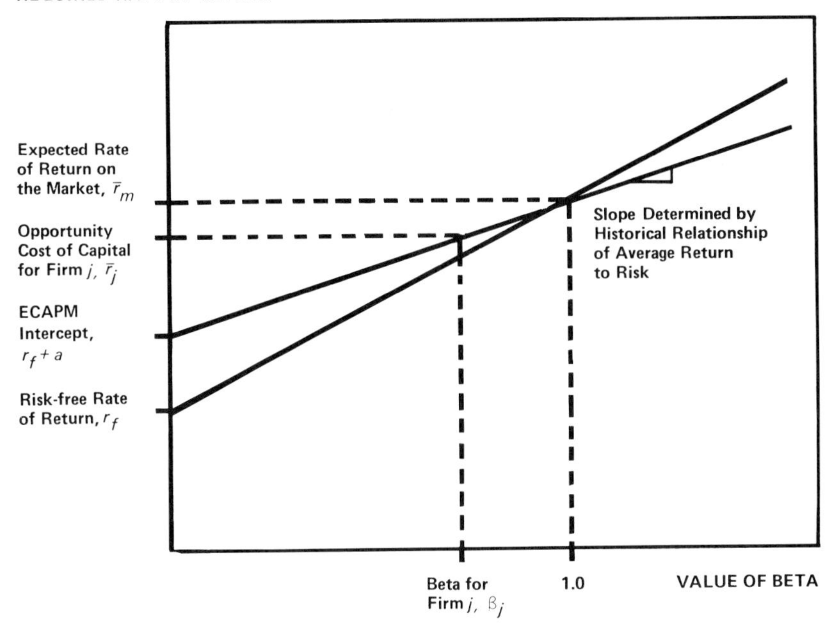

Figure 5.1
Application of Empirical CAPM

Evaluation

The ECAPM is an attempt at a practical solution for the problems arising when the assumptions of the CAPM seem violated, either because the CAPM theory is incomplete (for example, if investors consider skewness in fixing required rates of return) or because no way exists to implement the CAPM with available data (for example, if the missing assets in the "true" market portfolio, such as gold and houses, seriously bias the results found using only New York Stock Exchange data). The ECAPM collapses the various theoretical impacts of a number of such difficulties into two constants that can be estimated from market data. Whether this will turn out to be a useful approach in the long run depends on the stability of these two constants—whether the more complicated structure underlying these parameters is sufficiently constant over time.

The basic concept of reducing the complicated theoretical structure of an economic system to a simple form for econometric estimation is often used to make predictions. The strengths and problems of such "reduced form" predictions are well known. The strengths include computational simplicity, fewer delays while waiting for new data to be available, and accuracy of prediction *as long as the underlying theoretical structure is unchanged.* The chief weakness is that a change in the relationship of variables that are not explicitly included in the reduced-form equation can drastically change the "true" reduced form in a way that cannot be inferred from historical data. Predictions based on historical data are then invalid.

We do not know the full extent to which the ECAPM parameters, a and b, may be subject to such problems. However, some research bearing on this topic does exist. Black, Jensen, and Scholes 1972 and Fama and MacBeth 1973 find the parameters unstable when different short periods are used to estimate them, but this does not prove that the true underlying parameters are unstable. Over any short period, chance events might make low-beta stocks do better or worse than high-beta stocks, thereby biasing the estimate of b, even if in the long run the slope of the ECAPM line (i.e., b) were quite stable.

The natural response to the short-run chance fluctuations is to estimate a and b using data from a long period. If the true parameters are stable, this should work. The chance fluctuations will cancel out and the estimated parameters will be close to the true parameters.

But it is impossible to tell whether the long-period estimation has really solved the problem until one has two "long periods." Stability that can be discerned only over a long period can be confirmed only when the same parameters result from estimates over a subsequent long period. Thus it is difficult to predict when, if ever, statistical tests of the stability of the ECAPM parameters will prove sufficiently robust to resolve the issue.

Despite these reservations, ECAPM evidence should not be rejected out of hand. It is clearly possible that the true underlying parameters are sufficiently stable for the method's estimates to be valid. If this is true, alternative estimates made with the pure CAPM are likely to be wrong. Commissions should at least consider ECAPM evidence submitted today. We believe that approaches such as the ECAPM may eventually prove useful additions to the techniques used to estimate the cost of capital.

2. Pogue's Approach for Industries without Traded Stocks

Pogue 1979a estimates the cost of capital for oil pipelines, an industry in which virtually every company is the wholly owned subsidiary of a much larger company. His approach is novel in the way it uses accounting data to infer the relative risk of oil pipelines and the way it estimates the market risk-return line that determines the cost of capital given this risk. It may be useful in other applications where market data do not exist.

Definition and Assumptions

Pogue's approach uses accounting data to infer the beta of oil pipelines and then uses the estimated beta in a CAPM market-line equation to estimate the cost of capital for oil pipelines. Although Pogue separately estimates the security market line (equation [5.1]) in a novel way, his use of accounting data to infer beta in the absence of market data is the feature of particular interest in ratemaking applications.

Derivation of Oil Pipeline Beta

Pogue's procedures to derive a beta for oil pipelines rest on the assumption that the many biases in accounting data as estimates of true earnings affect only the *mean* of the estimated rate of return not the *variance* of that return. The justification for this assumption is as follows.

The mean of a series of N numbers, X_i, $i = 1, \ldots, N$, is calculated as

$$\overline{X} = \sum_{i=1.}^{N} \frac{X_i}{N} . \tag{5.3}$$

The variance of the series of numbers is calculated as

$$V = \sum_{i=1.}^{N} \frac{(X_i - \overline{X})^2}{(N - 1)} . \tag{5.4}$$

Together, equations (5.3) and (5.4) imply that the *variance* in book rates of return is likely to be a far better estimate of the variance in true rates of return than the *mean* book rate of return is of the mean true rate of return. For example, if each number is biased by a fixed amount, say B, the mean will be too large by amount B also. However, V will be entirely unaffected. This is easily verified by replacing X_i with $(X_i + B)$ in (5.3) and (5.4); the new mean is $(\overline{X} + B)$, but V is unchanged. More generally, the average bias in the values of X_i (if it is not constant for each number) will be removed in calculating the variance.

The implication is that unless the bias is made larger (or smaller) by larger true rates of return,[4] the variance of book rates of return is likely to be much closer to the variance of true rates of return than the mean book rate of return is to the mean true rate of return.

Pogue works with the standard deviation of accounting rates of operating income to total capitalization. (Standard deviation is the square root of the variance.) He estimates the standard deviations in book rates of return in two ways for two sample periods, for oil pipelines and for eighteen industries for which market data are available.

The two types of standard deviation are "cross-sectional," which measures the variability of accounting rates of return across a number of firms in a given industry, and "time series," which measures the variability in individual companies' accounting rates of return across time. The two periods were 1962–1976 and 1973–1977, selected because the necessary oil pipeline accounting data were available.

He next computes the beta of the eighteen reference industries, and "unlevers" the betas to remove the effects of financial risk (see appendix A for discussion of financial risk and how it affects the required rate of return). This step is necessary to prevent differences in financial structure from biasing the comparison.

The unlevering formula he uses is

$$\beta_U = \frac{\beta_L}{[1 + (1 - t) \times (D/E)],}$$

which translates as

$$\text{Unlevered beta} = \text{Observed stock market levered beta} \Big/ \left[1 + \left(1 - \text{Marginal corporate tax rate}\right) \times \left(\text{Market value of debt} \,/\, \text{Market value of equity}\right)\right].$$

He then calculates "best fit" lines (using least-squares regression analysis) to predict the value of beta using the value of each definition of the standard deviation of accounting returns for the eighteen industries. The best fit line is found by estimating parameters c and d in the equation $\beta_U = c + [d \times (\text{accounting standard deviation})]$.

Finally, by substituting the four standard deviations for oil pipelines into the four beta estimation equations, he obtains four

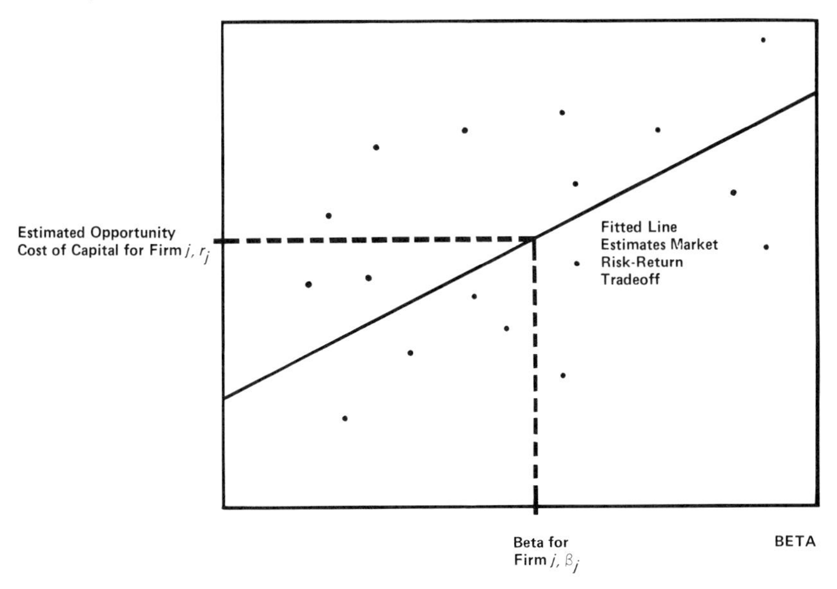

Figure 5.2
Pogue's Approach to Risk-Return Line

estimates of the betas of oil pipelines. He uses these four estimates to select a central value of beta for use in the market risk-return line.

Derivation of Market Risk-Return Line

This beta could have been used in the usual CAPM way, with a current estimate of the risk-free rate of return and an estimate of the market-risk premium based on historical averages over a long period. Pogue actually carries his analysis one more step, by estimating the market risk-return line itself in a novel way.

His procedure is to use Earnings Price Ratio and Discounted Cash Flow estimates of the cost of capital for a sample of 157 companies as the left-side variable in (5.1), and to estimate a constant (taking the place of the risk-free rate) and a coefficient of previously estimated betas for those companies on the right side. That is, he estimates constants a and b in the equation, $E(r_j) = a + (b \times \beta_j)$.[5] This procedure is pictured in figure 5.2 for the DCF estimate of the expected rate of return. Pogue averages the resulting two estimates a and b to obtain an equation for the CAPM market risk-return line and uses this equation and the oil pipeline beta estimated in the earlier step to find the cost of capital for oil pipelines.[6]

Evaluation

We believe that Pogue's procedures represent one sensible approach to the problem of missing market data.[7] The basic premise that the variability of book rates of return is far less subject to bias than the mean of book rates is sound. Pogue's procedures are not the only ones that might be used to derive an estimated cost of capital using accounting variability,[8] but he makes a reasonable attempt to fit the available data into the mainstream of current finance theory. The chief weakness of his approach is the amount of data analysis required. Also, the method's related costs are high because it is novel and involves several steps.

3. "Multifactor" Models

The last approach has not been used in rate-of-return testimony to our knowledge, but is worth mention as an indication of what the future may bring. This approach extends the form of (5.1) to include sensitivity to several factors other than the market-risk premium. Two paths to such an extension have been described in the financial literature: the "multi-beta" CAPM (MCAPM)[9] and the Arbitrage Pricing Theory (APT).[10] These approaches start from different premises and their authors appear to have different views on the "right" way to apply them. However, they can be shown to yield equations that look the same. Either might serve as the conceptual basis for rate-of-return testimony at some future date.

Definition and Assumptions

The formal development of these theories, especially the APT, is complicated, and the differences between them may be hard to grasp. We will concentrate on trying to provide an intuitive understanding of why a multifactor model may be appropriate and some notion of what form a multifactor equation might take.

The idea behind multifactor models is that more than the excess return on "the market" and a fixed sensitivity to that return (beta) may underlie the cost of capital. If the "true" factors underlying betas and the market-risk premium could be quantified, more exact estimates of the current cost of capital would be possible.

Specifically, the MCAPM can be interpreted as saying that a company's beta depends on a number of economic factors, and the degree to which these factors are important in determining market-wide returns may change over time. To express this sensitivity, betas with respect to each factor might be computed and the current importance of each factor considered in computing the current overall beta for the company.

The market as a whole seems sensitive to economic forces that change in importance over time, such as oil price shocks or inflation. Moreover, some stocks are more sensitive than others. When the uncertainty about such factors increases, the overall risk premiums of these sensitive companies would increase, depending on how responsive the market is to a change in the uncertainty of this factor.

The APT multifactor theory shows that under quite general assumptions, required rates of return will depend on the company's sensitivity to a number of factors, each of which has its own risk premium. This risk premium or the company's sensitivity to it may change over time. One of these factors may be "the market" as defined in the conventional CAPM, but it need not be. The market portfolio occupies no special place in the APT.[11] In contrast to the MCAPM, the economic interpretation of the factors underlying the APT cost of capital equation is deliberately left vague.[12]

Both the MCAPM and the APT can result in the same equation for how the cost of capital is determined (the variables in the equation have a somewhat different interpretation, which seems unlikely to have much practical impact if such an equation were used in rate-of-return testimony). If there are K factors in all, the equation is[13]

$$E(r_j) = r_f + [E(r_m) - r_f] \times (\gamma_1\beta_{j1} + \ldots + \gamma_K\beta_{jK}), \tag{5.5}$$

which translates as

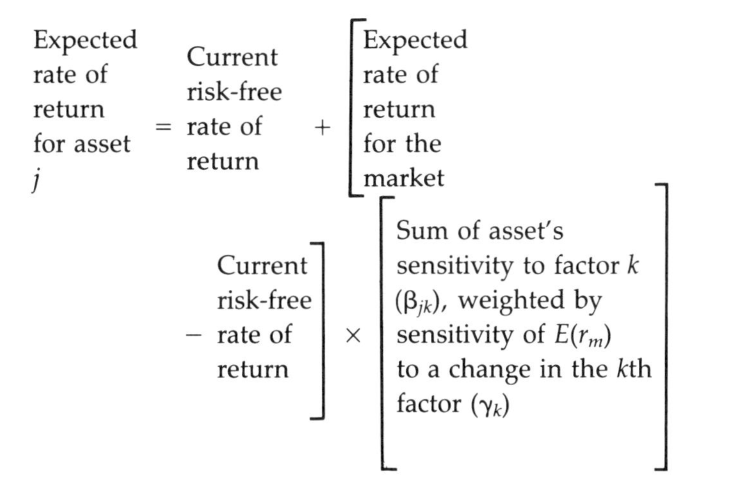

The sensitivity of the market to the various factors (the gammas—γ_ks) sum to one. If the market does not respond differently at different times because underlying economic forces are changing, there will be one gamma (equal to one), one beta, and (5.5) will be identical to (5.1), the original CAPM equation. If multiple risk factors are important, however, there will be more than one gamma *and* the relative size of gammas will be changing over time.[14]

Evaluation

Whether a witness will ever attempt to estimate the cost of capital using the APT, the MCAPM, or any similar multifactor model is an open question, as is the precise way in which such a model would be applied.[15] Detailed evaluation of multifactor models as a method of estimating the cost of capital is not possible at this time. But such models represent one important direction in which research on cost-of-capital formation is proceeding and add depth to the understanding of the CAPM.

4. Conclusion

The three techniques discussed in this chapter clearly are not the only ones that might come into use: we cannot claim to have reviewed more than a small fraction of the enormous volume of rate-of-return testimony available.

However, these three methods do share one important feature that we believe will be common to all useful new methods: they are grounded in the lessons of modern finance. In the last two decades there have been enormous gains in our understanding of risk and return in capital markets. Methods that do not recognize these new findings start with a serious disadvantage, and their findings should be suspect until it is clear how their assumptions relate to our current knowledge of finance.

The explosion of interest and research in finance makes life a lot harder for regulatory commissions and their staffs. No sooner is one technique mastered than another, supposedly superior technique comes along. Given the current level of research, it is safe to predict that this problem will persist for some time. Our hope is that we have provided the reader with sufficient understanding to judge the conflicting claims, to evaluate specific examples of rate testimony, and to feel confident when first encountering new approaches.

Appendix A The Effect of Debt on the Cost of Equity Capital

In most of this book we examine the cost of equity capital, since this is the major focus of testimony and debate. A brief summary of how debt and equity costs interact is needed to ensure that the estimated cost of equity capital is used correctly. The basic ideas presented here were first developed in the papers of Modigliani and Miller.

1. The Effect of Debt with No Market Distortions

Uncertainty about future operating earnings (earnings before interest and taxes) determines the business risk of a firm.[1] If a firm is financed entirely by equity capital, then stockholders will bear this risk only. If a firm is financed in part by debt capital, then stockholders will bear financial risk as well as business risk. Debt finance creates additional risk for stockholders because creditors have a prior claim on earnings. The degree of this financial "leverage" of operating earnings is summarized by the debt-equity ratio.

The principal conclusion of Modigliani and Miller 1958 is that in a world of frictionless capital markets and no taxes, the cost of capital is independent of leverage. The cost of equity capital, however, increases with leverage. Since the expected return on debt is lower than the expected return on equity, the cost of equity must rise as debt is substituted in order for the average cost of capital to be constant. But this result also follows from the principles of risk and return. Since debt finance increases the risk borne by stockholders, it increases the expected return on equity.[2]

This is pictured in figure A.1. The firm's overall cost of capital, r, is constant regardless of the firm's debt-equity ratio, (D/E).[3] As the share of debt increases, the cost of equity, r_e, increases also. If D/E becomes large enough, however, debtholders become exposed to

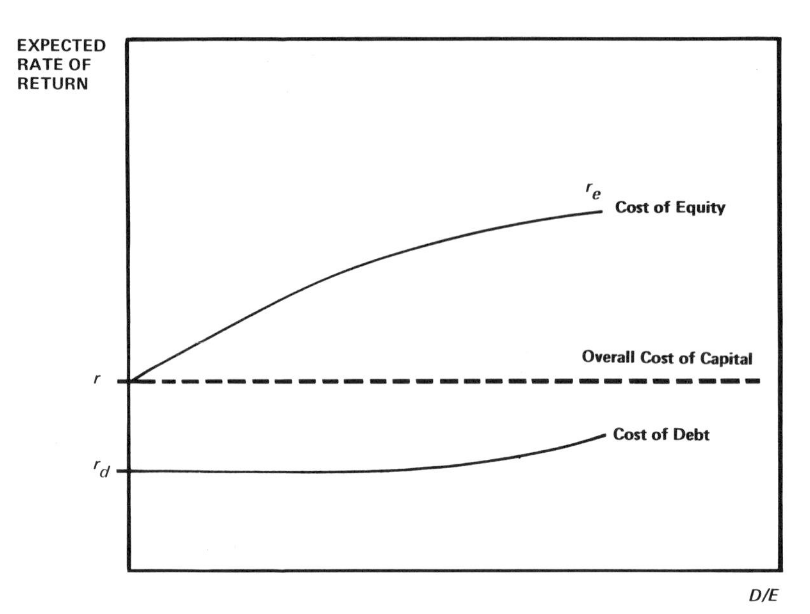

Figure A.1
Financial Risk and the Cost of Equity

significantly more risk. At this point, the cost of debt, r_d, begins to climb significantly and r_e climbs less rapidly, since debtholders are in effect shouldering some of the risks that equityholders bear at lower debt ratios.

This relationship may be summarized algebraically as[4]

$$r = \left[\left(\frac{D}{D + E}\right) \times r_d\right] + \left[\left(\frac{E}{D + E}\right) \times r_e\right], \tag{A.1}$$

which translates as

$$\begin{array}{l} \text{Firm's} \\ \text{overall} \\ \text{cost of} \\ \text{capital} \end{array} = \left[\begin{array}{l} \text{Share of} \\ \text{debt in} \\ \text{market} \\ \text{value of} \\ \text{firm's to-} \\ \text{tal assets} \end{array} \times \begin{array}{l} \text{Current} \\ \text{market} \\ \text{return to} \\ \text{debt (i.e.,} \\ \text{current} \\ \text{interest} \\ \text{rate)} \end{array}\right] + \left[\begin{array}{l} \text{Share of} \\ \text{equity} \\ \text{in firm's} \\ \text{total} \\ \text{assets} \end{array} \times \begin{array}{l} \text{Current} \\ \text{market} \\ \text{return to} \\ \text{equity} \\ \text{(i.e., cur-} \\ \text{rent cost} \\ \text{of equity} \\ \text{capital)} \end{array}\right].$$

Equation (A.1) confirms that since r is unaffected by adding debt, and r_d is less than r_e, r_e must increase to reflect increased financial risk.

Thus, given r, (A.1) shows how much financial risk increases the cost of equity, r_e. We can make this explicit by solving (A.1) for r_e:

$$r_e = r + (r - r_d)\frac{D}{E}. \tag{A.2}$$

Thus in the absence of taxes, two firms with identical business risks will have identical overall costs of capital, r, but will have different costs of equity capital if they are leveraged to different degrees.

2. The Effect of Debt with Market Distortions

The principal conclusions of the original Modigliani and Miller paper were derived in the context of idealized capital markets. They did not give explicit consideration to a number of factors that might influence the effect of debt on the cost of capital. A number of papers written since have explored some of these other factors in detail. The first significant extension was also by Modigliani and Miller, and considers corporate taxes.

Debt and Corporate Income Taxes

Equations (A.1) and (A.2) ignore the fact that interest expense is a deductible expense for corporate tax purposes. Using the same framework as their 1958 paper but including corporate income taxes, Modigliani and Miller 1963 conclude that the overall cost of capital is *not* independent of leverage.

Substituting debt for equity capital reduces the firm's taxes. This is a real saving to the firm, paid for by the federal government in the form of reduced tax receipts. Stockholders get the benefit of these savings, the value of which is the tax rate times interest expense.

The tax shield on debt thus reduces the cost of equity capital, r_e. We can express r_e in terms of r, the firm's overall cost of capital if it were *all-equity financed*. The "unlevered" cost of capital, r, depends only on business risk. If t is the *marginal* corporate income tax rate (the rate that would apply to additional earnings) the formula for r_e becomes[5]

$$r_e = r + (1 - t)(r - r_d)\frac{D}{E}. \tag{A.3}$$

Equation (A.3) implies that with taxes, the cost of equity will not rise as rapidly when the share of debt increases as it does without taxes.

Debt and Other Market Distortions

While adding the effect of corporate taxes was the main extension of the original theory, other important extensions also have been made.

One argument focuses on bankruptcy. The higher the degree of financial leverage, the greater the probability that a firm will find itself in bankruptcy. Since bankruptcy entails real costs, both tangible and intangible, the possibility of bankruptcy provides an offset to the corporate tax advantage of debt. It implies that the cost of capital is a minimum when the firm is less than 100-percent debt financed.

Another argument recognizes that although there is a corporate tax advantage to debt, there is a personal tax advantage to equity. In other words, if personal taxes are taken into account, the corporate tax advantage of debt is diminished. Farrar and Selwyn 1967 explore this point. Miller 1977 takes the observation a step further and develops an equilibrium theory. He concludes that there is an equilibrium debt ratio for the corporate sector of the economy, but that there is no optimal capital structure for the individual firm. His theory implies that there is no tax advantage to debt.[6]

More subtle arguments are based on the conflicts of interest among the claimants on the firm. Jensen and Meckling 1976 advance an argument based on the theory of agency. They observe that the divergences among the interests of owners, managers, and creditors give rise to agency costs. Principals and agents may expend resources to check these costs, but because these too are costly, there will be some residual losses. Optimal capital structure can be interpreted as a tradeoff between the costs of the divergences and the costs of monitoring and enforcing contracts.

Myers 1977 develops an argument for why certain kinds of firms borrow very little. He observes that part of the value of a firm consists of opportunities to make discretionary investments in the future. He further observes that if a firm has risky debt outstanding, there are circumstances in which it will be in the interests of stockholders to forego valuable investments. These circumstances arise only in the presence of risky debt, which in turn is due to financial leverage. Myer's argument implies that financial leverage entails very high costs for firms with substantial growth opportunities.

These are just some of the arguments that pertain to the corporate borrowing decision. Other authors find different reasons why the tax benefits are not as large as Modigliani and Miller 1963 suggest; for example, some firms cannot take advantage of all of their tax shields.

A complete enumeration of the pertinent arguments is beyond the scope of this appendix. The essential point is that a variety of factors tend to offset the apparent corporate tax advantage of debt financing, at least at very high levels of financial leverage.

The degree to which these factors influence the cost of capital is unclear. If the view that taxes are less important than (A.3) implies proves to be correct, (A.3) will have to be modified toward (A.2), so that r_e increases somewhat more rapidly as debt increases. See Myers 1983 for a nontechnical review of the current understanding of the effect of debt on a firm and Auerbach 1983 for a more technical survey with a somewhat different focus.

Special Issues under Rate-of-Return Regulation

Our inferences up to this point have assumed implicitly that we were discussing unregulated firms. The picture is somewhat more complicated for regulated firms. Most regulatory commissions treat both interest expense and income taxes as costs to be recovered from customers. Higher interest expense implies reduced income tax expense, and therefore lower rates than if equityholders were allowed to keep the benefits of the tax deductibility of interest. Since stockholders in regulated firms do not get to keep (the expected value of) the tax advantages of debt financing, how do the cost-of-capital equations presented above apply to regulated firms?

Usually, regulators pass the tax savings through to ratepayers by a reduction in the rate charged for each unit of service. In this case, *expected* operating revenues and operating income will be reduced by the amount of the tax shield, but *actual* operating income may be reduced by more or less, depending on whether customers buy more or less service than forecasted. In this case, equation (A.3) is correct for regulated firms if it is correct for unregulated firms (that is, if the effects of the factors other than corporate taxes are *not* important).[7] We use this case in the later numerical example.[8] However, given the current uncertainty over whether debt does reduce the overall cost of capital even for unregulated firms, we doubt that a serious mistake would be made if an expert chose to use (A.2) for a regulated firm.

3. Estimation of the Market Value of Debt

We must emphasize that regardless of whether (A.2) or (A.3) is used, D and E represent the *market*, not the book, value of the firm's outstanding debt and equity,[9] and that r_d is the current *market* interest rate the firm must pay for new debt. Even if regulators use a book value version of (A.1) and embedded interest rates (the original coupon rates on the firm's outstanding debt) in setting allowed revenues (that is, if they compute the so-called "weighted average cost of capital" for application to the firm's rate base), market value debt ratios and the current interest rate *must* be used if r_e is to be correctly adjusted for differences in financial risk.

The need to find market values does not pose a problem for equity. Common and preferred stock prices for publicly held companies can be found in the newspaper. Market value is just the price per share times the number of shares outstanding. Debt is another matter. The large number of debt issues by a single firm sometimes makes it difficult to compute market values. Moreover, many debt issues are not publicly traded at all. Although it is sometimes possible to value debt issue by issue, approximations are often necessary, especially when many companies are analyzed. We have found the following techniques helpful.

Book value is usually close to market value for short-term debt and for floating rate notes tied to current interest rates. Long-term debt is the main problem. Book value is sometimes used as an approximation for the market value of long-term debt, but book value exceeds market value more often than not. One reason is that interest rates have been well above normal in recent history. Many bond issues currently outstanding have very low coupons and therefore trade at low prices. The other reason is that most bonds have a call feature that allows the issuer to repurchase the bonds at an exercise price that is a little above par or face value. This applies to equity-linked debt (convertible bonds) since these, too, have call features that allow the issuers to repurchase bonds when prices rise much above par. Thus it is uncommon for bond prices to be far above book value.

One approach is for the analyst to calculate the average percentage discount of market from book value for a sample of issues and then apply this discount to the face value of all long-term debt. The analyst must be careful to choose bonds with comparable characteristics to the ones being valued. Relevant characteristics include maturity, coupon, call provisions, rating, and conversion features.

Also, a lower-bound estimate of market value may be obtained by capitalizing the net interest payments made by the firm at a current yield to maturity, r_d:

$$\text{Market value (lower-bound estimate)} = \frac{\text{Net interest expense (dollars per year)}}{r_d}$$

This treats debt as if it had infinite maturity—as if bondholders were stuck with low embedded interest forever. Since they are not, actual bond values exceed the lower-bound estimates. Nevertheless, such estimates are useful to establish the bottom of the range within which the true market value will fall (book value is usually taken as the top).

Alternatively, an average maturity (say, ten years) can be assumed and the market value estimated as the present value of the firm's current interest payments through that maturity date plus the redemption of the firm's outstanding bonds (at *book* value) at the end of that period. Again in this case, the current yield to maturity, r_d, is used as the discount rate in the present-value calculation.

However, if an extremely precise adjustment is desired, some cautions are in order when estimating the required rate of return on debt. The starting point over the remaining term of the instrument is the yield to maturity, but future changes in interest rates may prevent bondholders from reinvesting their coupon payments at this rate. Also, long-term rates are a complicated amalgam of short-term rates. The expected yield over any subperiod may differ significantly from the yield to maturity. Additionally, most bonds have some chance of default, which implies an *expected* return below the yield to maturity. In our view, however, use of the yield to maturity is acceptably accurate in the regulatory setting both for estimating the market value of debt and for use in equation (A.2) or (A.3).

4. Examples

Here is a balance sheet for Transylvania Electric.

Assets and net working capital	100	40	Debt
		60	Equity
Total assets	100	100	Total capitalization

We assume stock price equals book value per share and that bonds sell at par or face value. Thus there is no need for the moment to distinguish between book and market value (we relax this assumption at the end of the appendix). Suppose the fair rate of return on equity is 18 percent ($r_e = 0.18$). Now Transylvania Electric decides to move to a higher debt level, say to 60 percent debt and 40 percent equity. How does that change the fair return to equity?

From equation (A.3),

$$r_e = r + (r - r_d)(1 - t)\frac{D}{E}.$$

Suppose $t = 0.46$ and $r_d = 0.14$.[10] Thus

$$r_e = 0.18 = r + (r - 0.14)(1 - 0.46)\left(\frac{40}{60}\right).$$

This requires $r = 0.1694$. That is, if the firm had no debt, the fair return on equity would be 16.9 percent. Now calculate the fair rate of return on equity at the 60-percent debt level:

$$\underset{(60\%\ \text{debt})}{r_e} = r + (r - r_d)(1 - t)\frac{D}{E}$$

$$= 0.1694 + (0.1694 - 0.14)(1 - 0.46)\left(\frac{60}{40}\right)$$

$$= 0.1932 \text{ or } 19.3\%.$$

Table A.1 shows the fair rate of return to equity at a range of debt ratios. Note that the fair return to equity becomes extremely high as the firm approaches 100-percent debt financing. These returns reflect extremely high levels of financial risk. They do not impose an extra burden on consumers, however; as debt financing increases, the higher rate of return on equity is more than offset[11] by a reduction in the equity base to which it is applied.[12]

Table A.1
Fair rate of return to equity at a range of debt ratios

Debt as a percentage of total capitalization	Debt-to-equity ratio	Fair rate of return to equity (r_e)
0	0	0.169
10	1/9	0.171
25	1/3	0.175
40	2/3	0.180
50	1.0	0.185
60	1.5	0.193
80	4.0	0.232
90	9.0	0.312
95	19.0	0.471

As an example of another use of these principles, suppose we do not know r_e, the cost of equity capital for Transylvania Electric. However, assume r_e has been estimated for a group of companies with the same level of business risk but higher debt ratios. Suppose the average r_e for these companies is 0.185 and their average debt-equity ratio 1.0. Their current debt cost is $r_d = 0.14$. What is Transylvania's cost of equity? Again we use equation (A.3):

$$r_e = r + (r - r_d)(1 - t)\frac{D}{E}$$

$$0.185 = r + (r - 0.14)(1 - 0.46)\left(\frac{50}{50}\right).$$

This implies $r = 0.1694$, which is the appropriate rate of return for Transylvania Electric if it were all-equity financed. Since it is actually financed by 40 percent debt, the fair return is, as before,

$$\begin{aligned} r_e &= 0.1694 + (0.1694 - 0.14)(1 - 0.46)\left(\frac{40}{60}\right) \\ &= 0.18 \text{ or } 18\%. \end{aligned}$$

So far, we have assumed that Transylvania Electric's market and book balance sheets are the same. What happens if they are not? Suppose stock price is less than book value per share, so that the market debt ratio is higher than the book value. Specifically, assume:

	Book value	*Market value*
Debt	40	40
Equity	60	40
Debt-equity ratio	2/3	1.0

The expected rate of return on the *market* value of Transylvania's stock is 18.5 percent when $D/E = 1.0$.[13] Therefore, the fair rate at Transylvania's current, market debt-equity ratio is 18.5 percent. However, if it is allowed to earn this return on the *book* value of its equity, market price will increase, reducing the market debt-equity ratio and therefore the cost of capital.

The reason Transylvania's stock price is less than book value per share is that stockholders expect the firm's rate of return on equity to be too low. If a fair return is now allowed, stock price will increase. In fact, an 18.5-percent equity return will bring stock price above book value. The regulators will "overshoot" if they allow 18.5 percent and investors expect the firm to earn it.

We doubt this "overshooting" problem is serious in practice. If stock price rises significantly above book, an adjustment can be made in the next proceeding. If regulators wish to adjust before the fact, however, they should first calculate the debt-equity ratio consistent with a market price equal to book value, then allow a rate of return consistent with that debt-equity ratio. In this example, market equal to book implies $D/E = 2/3$ and $r_e = 0.18$, rather than 0.185 at $D/E = 1$. The adjustment is only 0.5 percentage points.

Thus, inequality of market and book values for actual companies poses no serious barrier to use of these equations.

5. Conclusions

The importance of debt for estimating the cost of equity capital in regulatory hearings is that the degree of leverage *must* be considered in applying the estimated cost of capital from another firm or industry to the regulated firm, or when hypothesizing changes in the firm's own debt-equity ratio. For example, "double leverage" testimony, in which the equity of a subsidiary is said to be part equity and part the debt of the parent, sometimes ignores how much financial risk the regulated firm would face if its equity were really the small percent that the double leverage argument implies. Also, a firm is sometimes said to use too little debt, and a higher debt ratio is imputed. If this is done, the cost of equity allowed to the firm must be increased to reflect the extra financial risk that equityholders would bear if the imputed debt ratio were really used by the firm.[14]

A properly computed measure of risk ought to measure both business and financial risk. The main text of this book focuses only on the cost of equity. However, the implications of this appendix must be remembered when comparing the cost of equity for different firms or industries.

Appendix B The Market-to-Book Ratio with "Vintaged" Equity Returns

The discussion of the market-to-book ratio in chapter 2 pointed out a fundamental inequity if regulated firms are forced to invest when their market-to-book ratio is below one: the regulated firm is then forced to make a new investment that is worth less to its shareholders than it costs. Unregulated firms are never exposed to such losses, because even if their stock's current market price is below book value, new investments will always have a market-to-book ratio at least equal to one.

Regulated firms are subject to such atypical losses because the entire equity share of their rate bases receives the same rate of return. To understand fully the implications of the market-to-book ratio for regulated firms, one should consider an alternative procedure: "vintaged" equity returns. This procedure sets the rate of return on the equity share of new investments once and for all at the time they are made, in the same way that conventional debt instruments have a fixed interest rate on their face value. If a commission were to adopt this procedure, the market-to-book value test would have to be modified, and failure to equate the firm's market and book values would no longer automatically imply that investors in regulated firms receive windfall gains or losses on each new investment.

We raise this topic for what it reveals about the nature and merits of the market-to-book test, not because we believe vintaging equity returns is desirable. To reinforce this point and to assure that the discussion is not misleading, we will mention some of the adverse consequences of adopting this procedure.

1. The Mechanics and Lessons of Vintaged Equity

The notion of vintaged equity returns is straightforward. Each time new investments are made, the commission estimates the cost of capital for the equity share of the investment. This cost of capital is applied to the net book value of this investment's equity share as long as it remains in the rate base, so that the rate of return to equity becomes the average of the rates of return to the various investment vintages, weighted by their current share of the rate base.[1]

The commission still has the problem of finding the cost of capital for each new investment. The difference is that it is applied only to the new equity not to the entire rate base. Therefore, the pros and cons of the various cost-of-capital estimation methods are equally relevant with a vintaging approach. Vintaging saves no efforts in estimating the required rate of return.

The market-to-book test is still relevant but is applied only to the *new* investment's equity. What is being compared is the increment in total market value to the increment in the rate base, rather than the total market value to the total rate base. The commission knows it has set a rate of return equal to the current cost of capital if the total market value of all shares outstanding increases by the book value of the equity share of the addition to the rate base. Thus, vintaging avoids the windfall gains and losses on new investments that occur under current procedures when the market-to-book ratio differs from one.

The holdings of existing investors (the owners of the earlier vintages) are unaffected by new investments; if they were selling below (or above) book value before the new investment (because the cost of capital had increased or decreased since the earlier vintages were added), they will be selling the same amount below (or above) book value after the new investment, if regulators estimate the cost of capital on the new investment correctly.

The implication of these results is that the current use of the market-to-book test for the total value of the company implies that the average, not just the incremental, rate of return on equity will equal the cost of capital. All of the regulated firm's equity investors expect to find their returns keeping pace with current capital market conditions, not just new investors.

2. Drawbacks of Vintaged Equity

A vintaging procedure may produce a number of undesirable effects.

First, the firm's equity would become analogous to a conventional bond, but with far less certainty about the amount that will actually be earned each year.[2] Vintaged equity would tend to combine the worst aspects of both stocks and bonds: the expected return would be fixed regardless of changes in current interest rates, like conventional bonds, but the realized return would be as uncertain as any other utility stock's, in that unforeseen changes in forecasted expenses and sales could make actual returns considerably different from expected returns.

Investors in all likelihood would require a higher rate of return on new capital as a result. This could cost customers considerably more than they save, especially if the reverse in the upward trend in the cost of capital in the 1970s and early 1980s continues, or if it is replaced by fluctuations around a steady mean value.

Fluctuations in capital costs would create other problems as well. For example, when costs of capital decline, regulators and customers would be locked in to paying rates of return on equity that are well above the then-current levels required.

Also, there would be an increased administrative burden from the need to keep track of the current equity rate-base share of each asset vintage. This burden could be large; for example, depreciation would have to be accumulated for each year's investments, not just in total.

Implementation of equity vintaging would be especially difficult. Even if a commission wished to start vintaging new equity, vintaged returns were not part of the implicit contract with regulators when *past* investments were made. Vintaging on future assets does not affect the general obligation to let today's investor expect to receive the current cost of capital. Old assets should therefore continue to receive the current cost of capital at the same time that new assets are vintaged. The administrative burden would be heavy.

Our discussion of vintaged equity reveals that the market-to-book test works well for each addition to the asset base, not merely for total assets. As a potential regulatory policy, however, equity vintaging would have some serious problems.

Appendix C Technical Notes on the Empirical Analysis

1. Data Sources

Financial data for the sample of regulated and unregulated companies were provided to CRA by Professor Gerald Pogue of the City University of New York. These data, prepared by Pogue for the Federal Energy Regulatory Commission, were numbers he calculated from raw data in the *Compustat* database.

Interest rates were obtained from publications of the Federal Reserve System, including the *Federal Reserve Bulletin* (for the most recent data) and the *Annual Statistical Digest*. The yields on one-, three-, and five-year government notes are reported in table A.27 of the *Bulletin*, and a historical summary of this series is provided in the *Digest*.

The return on equity for the Standard & Poor's industrial index was constructed from data reported in the 1979 Standard & Poor's *Analyst's Handbook*. More recent data were obtained from the Standard & Poor's *Current Statistics*. The return on equity reported in our study is the ratio of earnings per share to book value per share.

2. Selection of Company Sample

The sample of company data originally supplied us by Pogue included approximately 350 companies. The companies actually included in our empirical work were selected by a two-stage process.

We eliminated companies with missing observations in the 1971 to 1980 period. To have included companies with missing observations would have raised the problem of having, say, six firms in an industry sample in one year, then eight in another year. Missing observations were common since several of the data series were averages (or trends) of five or ten years of data.

The group of companies that passed this initial screening were then grouped by two-digit SIC code (the Standard Industrial Classification system of the Department of Commerce). A total of seventeen groups was thereby formed. We arbitrarily eliminated industry groups that consisted of less than six companies. Eleven industry groups remained, one consisting of electric utilities and ten unregulated groups.

3. Computational Procedures

The cost of equity for an industry group was calculated by first estimating the cost of equity for the companies that comprised that group and then computing the average of these company estimates. For example, suppose an industry group consisted of three companies, and suppose that the DCF estimates of the cost of equity for those companies were 10, 20, and 15 percent, respectively. Then the industry DCF cost of equity would be equal to 15 percent.

DCF estimates of the cost of equity were calculated by the formula

$$k = \left(\frac{D}{P}\right)(1 + g) + g,$$

where k is the cost of equity, D/P is the company dividend yield on year-end stock price, and g is the growth rate. The three DCF estimates were obtained by substituting the alternative growth rates, $G1$, $G2$, $G3$, for g. The dividend yield on common stock is equal to the ratio of annual dividends per share to the closing stock price on the last trading day of the year.

The three DCF growth rates were computed as follows. The "trend" growth rates were estimated by the ordinary least-squares regression of the logarithm of earnings per share on a time trend. The ten-year trend, $G1$, in 1975, for example, would have used earnings per share for 1966 through 1975. The five-year trend, $G2$, would have used data for 1971 through 1975. The "sustainable growth" rate, $G3$, was calculated by the five-year average return on equity times the five-year average retention rate of earnings. The retention rate is equal to one minus the ratio of dividends to earnings.

The earnings-price method cost of equity, PE, was calculated as the ratio of annual earnings per share to the closing stock price on the last trading day of the year.

The five-year average return on equity, *ROE*, was calculated as the simple average of the return on equity for the most recent five years. Thus, for 1978 the *ROE* would equal the average of the return on equity for the years 1974 through 1978.

CAPM estimates of the cost of equity were calculated by the formula

$$k = \text{INT3} + \text{BETA} \times (9.2),$$

where INT3 is the yield on three-year government notes and BETA is the beta coefficient, and 9.2 percent is the market risk premium estimated by Ibbotson & Sinquefield 1977. The beta coefficient was estimated by the ordinary least-squares regression of common stock returns on the returns on the Standard & Poors composite index (the S&P 500).

The dividend yields, growth rates, betas, and average *ROE*s were calculated by Pogue and supplied to us directly. We did not have access to the raw data in the *Compustat* database.

4. Companies in the Electric Utility Sample

The 36 companies included in the electric utility sample are:

Allegheny Power Sys. Inc.

American Electric Power Inc.

Atlantic City Electric Company

Boston Edison Company

Carolina Power & Light

Central & South West Corporation

Central Maine Power Company

Cleveland Electric Illum. Company

Commonwealth Edison

Detroit Edison Company

Duke Power Company

Duquesne Lt. Company

El Paso Elec. Company

Florida Power & Light Company
Florida Power Corporation
General Public Utilities Corporation
Gulf States Utilities Company
Hawaiian Electric Inc.
Houston Inds. Inc.
Idaho Power Company
Indianapolis Power & Light Company
Kansas City Power and Light Company
Kansas Gas & Electric Company
Kentucky Utilities Company
Middle South Utilities Inc.
Minnesota Power & Light Co.
Nevada Power Co.
New England Elec. Sys.
Ohio Edison Company
Oklahoma Gas & Electric
Pennsylvania Power & Light Company
Potomac Electric Power Company
Public Service Company of Indiana, Inc.
Public Service Company of New Hampshire
Public Service Company of New Mexico
Puget Sound Power & Light Company

Notes

Chapter 1

1. As this is written, there is great relief that inflation is "only" about four percent annually, a level viewed as totally unacceptable in the 1950s and '60s.

2. This differs from the third problem in asserting that the allowed rate of return itself is too low. The third problem says that realized earnings fall short of allowed earnings.

3. A procedure like this has (apparently) been used by the New Mexico Public Service Commission.

4. This indexing procedure was one of those discussed by the Staff Study Group, U.S. Federal Energy Regulatory Commission 1980. Since that study the FERC has instituted a procedure for establishing a "benchmark" rate of return (Docket no. RM80-36).

5. Such a procedure was discussed in Myers 1979, and may have contributed to the FERC's decision to retain a modified form of rate-base trending for oil pipelines. (A recent court decision has sent the issue back to the FERC.) A similar system, similarly motivated, is in the process of adoption by the Interstate Commerce Commission for railroads. The advantages and difficulties are worked out in more detail in Myers, Kolbe, and Tye (forthcoming); several ways to deal with the problems of inflation-driven rate shocks, including rate of return indexing and rate base trending, are compared in Kolbe 1983. See also Navarro, Peterson, and Stauffer 1981 and Charles River Associates 1984b.

6. See Hughes 1983, Hyman 1983, Joskow & Schmalensee 1983, Plummer 1983, and Schweppe 1983.

7. "Flow-through" of the benefits of accelerated depreciation sets allowed tax expense equal to actual taxes paid. "Normalization" of these benefits sets allowed tax expense at what actual taxes would have been without accelerated depreciation, usually with an accompanying reduction in the company's rate base. The Economic Recovery Tax Act of 1981 requires normalization if utilities are to use the greatly accelerated recovery of capital

costs it permits, and so for the moment has largely eliminated this source of controversy.

8. "Working" capital refers to the money balances needed to conduct the day-to-day transactions of the company. An allowance for working capital is typically included as a part of the rate base, as is the cost of the financial capital used during the construction of the physical capital.

9. In computing the revenue requirement, commissions typically allow as an expense the actual interest outlays by the company, rather than the current required rate of return on the current market value of the company's outstanding debt. The amount allowed corresponds to the sum of the differing coupon payments to the different bonds issued by the company over the years. For equity, on the other hand, the goal is to allow the same current required rate of return for all of the company's outstanding equity.

10. "Cost of capital" in this phrase is *not* the same thing as "cost of capital" as it is used elsewhere in this book. The "weighted average cost of capital" in regulation is defined as the allowed rate of return on the utility rate base. The "cost of capital" in finance is defined in chapter 2.

Chapter 2

1. To ensure a common background, this chapter restates a number of standard principles in the field of finance. Leading textbooks in the field include Weston and Brigham 1983, Copeland and Weston 1983, Van Horne 1983, and Brealey and Myers 1984. We refer to the last of these when a more detailed discussion of a particular point may be helpful.

2. Factors other than risk, such as liquidity and tax status, may affect the cost of capital for some investments. We confine our attention to the cost of equity capital, and risk is the main characteristic that distinguishes equity investments.

3. This principle does not hold in all circumstances. If a company is in financial distress, the cost of capital for a particular investment undertaken by that company might exceed the cost of capital for that investment undertaken by companies not in financial distress. See Brealey and Myers 1984, chapter 18, for a discussion of financial distress and its attendant costs. Our discussion assumes that the firm is not in financial distress.

4. Because inflation makes the purchasing power of monetary assets uncertain, investors bear some risk even when buying Treasury bills. However, Treasury bills are close to risk free even in "real" (constant dollar) terms, because near-term inflation can be predicted with reasonable accuracy. Treasury bills thus provide an analytical benchmark for understanding how security prices are established in capital markets.

5. The possibility of a changed slope for the market line is one argument sometimes advanced (at least implicitly) in a regulatory hearing to make the

case for a "negative risk premium" between the costs of debt and utility equity. As discussed briefly in the risk positioning section of chapter 3, we find little or no merit in the arguments advanced for a negative risk premium.

6. The first of these looks like the "weighted average cost of capital" defined in the regulatory sense of chapter 1. However, it is not the same, because D, E, and r_d are market, not book, values. See appendix A.

7. The seminal article on the use of the cost of capital in public utility rate hearings is Myers 1972b.

8. *Bluefield Water Works v. P.S.C.*, 262 U.S. 679 (1923); *F.P.C. v. Hope Natural Gas Co.*, 320 U.S. 591 (1944).

9. *Federal Power Commission v. Hope Natural Gas Company* 320 U.S. 591 at 603 (citation omitted). The act to which the court refers is the Natural Gas Act of 1938. This statute contains language about the establishing of rates for regulated utilities similar to the language in most public utilities legislation. *Hope* speaks of *return* to investors, not the *rate of return on equity*. However, it is generally accepted that the legal standards for returns also apply to rate of return on equity determinations.

10. *Hope* at 602; *F.P.C. v. Natural Gas Pipeline Co.*, 315 U.S. 575 and 586 (1942); *Conway* Corporation 6, F.P.C., 510, F. 2d. 1264 at 1274 (D.C. Cir.), affirmed, 426 U.S. 271 (1975); *Montana-Dakota Utilities Co. v. Northwestern Public Service Co.*, 341 U.S. 246 at 251 (1950).

11. *Hope* at 602; *Natural Gas Pipeline* at 586; *Southwestern Bell Telephone Co. v. Public Service Commission*, 262 U.S. 276 at 291 (1923); *Chicago N.W.R. Co. v. A.T.&S.F.R. Co.*, 387 U.S. 326 at 347 (1967).

12. *Permian Basin Area Rate* Cases, 390 U.S. 747 at 769-770 (1968).

13. *Town of Alexandria, Minnesota*, U.F.P.C., 555, F. 2d. 1020 at 1028 (D.C. Cir., 1977).

14. *Borough of Fellwood City v. FERC*, 583, F. 2d. 642 at 649 (3rd Cir., 1978).

15. This issue is frequently raised by discussing the "dilution" of the existing stockholder's shares when new stock is sold for less than the book value of existing shares.

16. A series of articles in the economics literature argues that investors will use too much capital relative to other factors of production if they are allowed more than their cost of capital. This increases the cost to customers, wasting resources through inefficient production techniques. See Averch and Johnson 1962, Baumol and Klevorick 1970, Bailey and Coleman 1971, and Bailey 1973.

17. These concepts of fairness seem to underlie the concept of a "balance" of customer and producer interests necessary for the fair "end result" in the *Hope* decision.

18. See Kolbe 1983 for examples of rate-of-return indexing procedures that accomplish this goal.

19. The excess is intended to offset the cost of issuing new stock. For simplicity, the remainder of the discussion ignores issue costs and speaks only of a market-to-book ratio equal to one. However, commissions basing policy on the market-to-book ratio should consider issue costs as well. See Arzac and Marcus 1981 for one discussion of how this should be done. Bierman and Hass 1984 advocate a different approach.

20. Stockholders need not plan to hold their stock indefinitely. Its sales price to a new investor will equal its present value at that time, which depends on all future expected earnings as of that date.

21. The appropriate standard is not clear in Fair Value jurisdictions. If a Fair Value rate of return were chosen in conjunction with the Fair Value rate base to produce the same earnings in every year as would have resulted under Original Cost and a conventional rate-of-return determination, the jurisdiction would effectively be under Original Cost and the market-to-book ratio could be interpreted in the standard way discussed earlier. Our conversations with regulatory staff members suggest that this is often the case, but we have made no formal survey. In contrast, under a Trended Original Cost methodology, which defines the fair rate or current earnings in real terms and allows rate-base write-ups to reflect inflation, market value should be compared to the written-up rate base, not to book value. For discussions of alternatives to the usual rate-base methodology, see Myers 1979, Navarro, Peterson, and Stauffer 1981, and Myers, Kolbe, and Tye (forthcoming).

22. Some utilities have recently been allowed to include CWIP in their rate bases but this is not currently standard practice.

23. One reason AFUDC is sometimes referred to as "low quality" earnings may be that investors in fact do *not* expect to earn the cost of capital on this amount, so that the present value of the earnings investors do expect is lower than the AFUDC recorded on the books.

24. See Modigliani and Cohn 1979, Feldstein 1980, Fama 1981, and Hendershott 1981, among others.

25. This statement refers to a basic change in tax rates, not to issues such as normalization versus flow-through of accelerated depreciation charges.

26. Joskow 1974 argues that utility investors may have systematically earned more than their cost of capital in the 1960s because regulators did not reduce rates in spite of declining costs resulting from productivity increases and low rates of general inflation. Even if his argument is correct, it seems doubtful that this experience could be repeated. Nor is a two-decade-long "averaging out" of the rate of return and the cost of capital desirable, if sensible investment decisions are to be made.

27. Note that financing new investments with debt does *not* avoid the burden on shareholders unless regulators simultaneously allow at least enough of an increase in the allowed return on equity to compensate for the increased financial risk—unless the market-to-book ratio falls no farther when the new

debt is issued. If the market-to-book ratio is allowed to remain below one, the burden can be avoided in the long run only by allowing a different equity rate of return on new assets versus old assets. A separate equity rate of return would have to be allowed for each vintage of regulated assets. While technically feasible, adoption of such a policy would create serious problems. See appendix B for discussions of how this vintaging concept relates to the market-to-book ratio and of the serious drawbacks to this concept as a regulatory policy.

28. This statement applies to use of the market-to-book ratio as a *test* of whether the rate of return equals the cost of capital. As will be discussed in chapter 3, problems can arise when the market-to-book ratio is used to estimate the cost of capital itself.

29. The market-to-book ratio can fall no further than zero but can rise indefinitely, giving an exaggerated visual importance to the values above unity in figure 2.4. The logarithmic scale of figure 2.5 provides visual symmetry to shortfalls and overages: a market-to-book ratio of 0.5 is just as large a deviation below 1.0 as is a market-to-book ratio of 2.0 is above 1.0. (The logarithm of 1.0 is 0.0, so ratios below 1.0 are negative in figure 2.5 and ratios above 1.0 are positive.)

30. See Myers, Kolbe, and Tye (forthcoming), Kolbe 1983, and CRA 1984b.

31. It is easy to construct examples in which a 3-percent change in the rate of growth of unregulated prices requires a 25-percent increase in the return to equity, or where the first year's electric rates for a new nuclear power plant would be 30- to 50-percent lower if the regulatory system mimicked unregulated prices (see Kolbe 1983).

32. It is worth noting that there are two approaches to remedying a low market-to-book ratio: increase the allowed rate of return to equal the cost of capital; or decrease the risks to which investors are exposed, thereby reducing the cost of capital toward the allowed rate of return. Cost indexing arrangements such as fuel-adjustment clauses can have this effect, but the persistence of the low market-to-book ratios suggests that such risk-reduction strategies did not solve the problem. Also, indexing can encourage poor practices by removing some incentives for efficiency.

Chapter 3

1. Lord Keynes's famous statement comes to mind: "Practical men, who believe themselves to be quite exempt from any intellectual influences, are usually the slaves of some defunct economist" (Keynes 1965, p. 383).

2. Interest rates differ for bonds maturing at different dates (rates for bonds to be redeemed in one year will differ from those to be redeemed in thirty years). The most appropriate time to maturity for the comparative interest rate is probably that which matches the period for which the company's rates are to be in effect.

3. The true rate of return equals the cash flow plus the change in the economic value of the firm's assets over the year, divided by the initial value of the assets.

4. For example, if true rates of return and costs of capital were always two percentage points higher than book rates of return for both regulated and unregulated firms, equating book rates of return would equate true rates of return. Of course, this line of argument also requires that the average past true rate of return earned by the comparable-risk firms equals their current cost of capital.

5. Another way that the CE approach can fail the logical consistency test is if the comparable-risk sample consists of other regulated firms. This makes the CE method circular: the data needed to apply the method become contaminated by its use.

6. We neglect a third problem. The sample of comparable-risk firms may be incorrectly chosen. This problem is less fundamental than the first two.

7. See Holland and Myers 1979 and 1980.

8. The use of a long sample period requires one to address another issue: Was the cost of capital stable throughout the sample period?

9. This statement is not strictly true. The conservatism principle requires that when there is a choice between two values, the lower value should be chosen. The application of this principle to current assets, for example, results in the rule that marketable securities should be reported at the lower of cost or market value. But notice that this rule does not allow asset values to be revised upward. Appreciation in asset values (from inflation, for example) is not recognized.

10. Nominal earnings include gains from inflation, while real earnings deduct gains from inflation.

11. Examples similar to that in table 3.2 could be constructed where inflation leads to overestimates of the true rate of return.

12. Fisher and McGowan 1983, pp. 83, 97 (emphasis added).

13. See Myers 1979, Myers, Kolbe, and Tye (forthcoming), or Navarro, Peterson, and Stauffer 1981 for analysis of alternative rate-base concepts.

14. An attempt to conduct a rigorous study using accounting returns is Holland and Myers 1979 and 1980, who used the national income accounts to examine the real rates of return on all United States nonfinancial corporations in the period since World War II. These authors explicitly compare their results with evidence from capital markets, to test whether their application of accounting data seems reasonable.

15. Familiarity with the CE method is clearly an advantage only when the witness's goal is to equate book rates of return regardless of whether this implies a rate of return equal to the cost of capital. As noted at the outset, we assume that this is *not* the relevant goal.

16. Planned resale by the initial investor does not upset the DCF model, because the expected sale price would reflect the discounted value of subsequent dividends.

17. This is just the reciprocal of the price-earnings ratio reported with stock prices in the newspaper.

18. Note that the EPR is *not* the same as estimating the dividend growth rate using the "sustainable growth" approach. That approach estimates g as the ratio of retained earnings to the *book* value of equity. (The two will be the same only if the market-to-book ratio equals one or if $g = 0$—if the firm is not growing at all.)

19. For example, see Brealey and Myers 1981, chapter 4.

20. The present value of a perpetual steady cash flow is the cash flow divided by the cost of capital, as can be seen by setting $g = 0$ in (3.3).

21. We ignore the possibility that some firms might be willing to operate indefinitely at substandard earnings. Managers of such firms would not be acting in the interest of stockholders.

22. This leads to the same logical consistency problem that the Market-to-Book Ratio approach has when the firm's own stock price is used.

23. See any econometrics textbook for a description of ordinary least-squares regression methods. Computer software to compute regressions is readily available. Even some hand-held calculators have this capability.

24. This problem might be remedied by using deflated (inflation-adjusted) historical data in deriving DCF estimates. Gottstein 1983 compares this method to other ways of calculating DCF estimates.

25. Biases in DCF estimates associated with regulatory lag, and in general with investors' attempts to predict future regulatory behavior, are mitigated if the DCF estimates are based on a broad sample of equivalent-risk firms rather than on data just for the firm being regulated. Our example assumes a single firm in order to dramatize the problems DCF estimates can run into.

26. When we refer to the CAPM we usually mean the Sharpe-Lintner capital asset pricing model. There have been numerous extensions of the Sharpe-Lintner model.

27. Finance theory has not yet answered this question fully. The discussion in this section is based on mean-variance portfolio analysis, which provides at least one important part of the answer.

28. The variance of a random variable is the expected value of the squared deviation of the random variable from its mean; algebraically, this is the expected value of $(X - \overline{X})^2$ where $\overline{X}$ is the mean of random variable X. The standard deviation is the square root of the variance.

29. Beta is usually defined in another, equivalent way; we believe the explanation on this page provides a better intuitive grasp of the concept.

30. Note, however, that many billions of dollars are invested in "index funds," which track the performance of the overall market with excellent fidelity. Such funds offer maximum diversification, average performance, and low management fees.

31. Experts whose procedures lead to quite different results from betas computed in conventional ways should be expected to explain in detail both the rationale for their method and why its results are different.

32. See Kolbe 1983 for examples of the possible size of these fluctuations and for discussion of ways to reduce their impacts.

33. Actually, Merton used the Ibbotson and Sinquefield data base published in 1979; updates on this data base are now frequently published and widely used.

34. The returns on Treasury bills (r_f) are typically uncorrelated with the returns on the market (r_m). As a practical matter, therefore, the same estimate of beta is usually obtained by regressing r_j on r_m and neglecting the interest rate term.

35. As noted, more complicated ways of calculating beta are sometimes used, including weighting more recent data more heavily and adjusting the observed beta toward one.

36. The geometric mean rate of return equals the *n*th root of the product of one plus the actual rates of return over *n* years, minus one. It may also be worth noting that Merton 1980 derives his alternative estimates of the market risk premium by different assumptions about the way investors view risk, not by use of the geometric mean.

37. A more detailed discussion of this issue is in the *Instructor's Manual* to Brealey and Myers 1981.

38. As noted above, use of short-term bond rate can lead to unstable estimates of the cost of equity, so the yields on long-term bonds are sometimes used instead. This alternative procedure gives a more stable but less accurate estimate of the current cost of capital and the allowed rate of return. (See Kolbe 1983.)

39. We should also note that Black 1972 shows that limitations on investor borrowing may imply that the intercept of the market line on the vertical axis exceeds the risk-free rate. The Black intercept is the return on a "zero-beta portfolio."

40. Regressions to estimate a stock's beta produce an estimated value for alpha in the sample period, but this is an *ex post* measurement. It can be interpreted as the average performance of the stock above or below the CAPM prediction during the sample period. It is not a good estimate of expected stock-specific performance over and above the market factor in future periods, because investors will have capitalized the relevant information in the past alpha in the current stock price.

41. The inclusion of alpha by no means resolves all of the criticisms of the CAPM theory. Some critics develop alternative theories, some of which we discuss in chapter 5. For present purposes, however, the reasons that alpha may be needed suffice to illustrate the criticisms of the CAPM theory.

42. Banz 1981 and Reinganum 1981a report evidence of the small firm effect. That evidence has been challenged by Roll 1981 and Brown, Kleidon, and Marsh 1983.

43. For example, see Litzenberger and Ramaswamy 1979. Their preferred model equation is actually somewhat different from (3.10). However, it would imply a positive alpha for high-dividend firms. Miller and Scholes 1982 have challenged Litzenberger and Ramaswamy's tests.

44. See Kraus and Litzenberger 1976, and Friend and Westerfield 1980.

45. CRA 1984a demonstrates that this is a serious problem for estimation of betas for electric utilities, operating telephone companies, and natural gas-distribution companies. These results show that utility betas (adjusted to be comparable to traditional betas) are higher when estimated using a "market" index that includes stocks and bonds than when estimated on the stock market alone, while the adjusted betas of comparison unregulated industries are unaffected. The CRA 1984a findings may also have relevance for the "dividend controversy" over whether high-dividend stocks receive appropriate returns for their risk; the risk estimates (betas) used in some studies of the dividend controversy are likely to be too low for public utilities, which are a high proportion of the market value of high-dividend stocks.

46. It would probably be useful to a commission if a witness who did use the original CAPM were to supplement his or her testimony by showing how the results would change if some of the criticisms of the Sharpe-Lintner CAPM are valid. However, such supplemental information would add to the costs and complexity of CAPM testimony.

47. Again, this is the yield to maturity, not the percent that the coupon payment is of the face or current market value of the bond.

48. The difference in interest rates between AAA and A bonds is often on the order of one percentage point.

49. Merton 1980 is the only paper we know of that reports numerical results on this topic, although CRA (forthcoming) reports an unsuccessful empirical attempt to obtain such results.

50. Applications of the Capital Asset Pricing Model also assume a constant market-risk premium. Our previous discussion of this assumption carries over to the RP approach. Our conclusion also carries over, namely that use of a constant risk premium is probably reasonable for ratemaking purposes.

51. See Bodie 1976 and Fama and Schwert 1977.

52. This is not a problem under some of the proposed changes in regulatory

procedures, in particular use of a trended instead of an original cost rate base. See Myers, Kolbe, and Tye (forthcoming).

53. The DCF method might get around this problem if the variation described earlier, to estimate the real cost of capital and then add the current inflation premium, were followed.

54. See Kolbe 1983 for a comparison of alternative methods to accommodate this problem.

55. Of course, more complex ways of finding the risk premium increase the related costs.

56. Market value should actually exceed book value by a small amount, to cover the costs of issuing the stock. This chapter's discussion ignores this excess and speaks only of a market-to-book ratio equal to one. An adjustment for issue costs is necessary in practice. See Arzac and Marcus 1981 and Bierman and Hass 1984 for discussions of how to compute the adjustment.

57. Again, a slight excess over one is needed to cover stock issuance costs.

58. The biased coefficient occurs because today's returns are smaller than the returns investors *expect*, so the least-squares regression coefficient of *today's* returns will be larger than the true coefficient for expected returns, as the regression attempts to "explain" the observed variability of the market-to-book data.

59. A more exact formula using continuous compounding and the expected dividends flowing from the allowed earnings (including their exact timing) should be used if a commission actually wanted to apply this approach.

Chapter 4

1. The estimated standard deviation for the estimated mean of the underlying distribution is the estimated standard deviation of the annual returns (in this case, 21.9 percent) divided by the square root of the number of observations in the sample (in this case, 56). By the central limit theorem, a 95-percent confidence interval for the estimated mean is approximately plus or minus two standard deviations around the mean.

2. We are indebted to Gerald Pogue for supplying much of the data we use.

3. It is possible to observe the cost of debt because the amount and timing of interest payments are fixed. Common stock dividends, in contrast, change with time in an unspecified way.

4. In other words, we used equally weighted portfolios of stocks. A somewhat better procedure would have been to use value-weighted portfolios, in which the weights are equal to the relative market values of the equities. Unfortunately, the format in which our data set was provided precluded this.

5. Comparable earnings estimates for *regulated* industries are circular: a mis-

take by regulators in one year will not be self-correcting but will lead to mistakes in subsequent years as well. Ten of the eleven industry groups are unregulated.

6. Estimates of the market risk premium based on more recent data differ from this but not by a great deal. Alternative estimates would affect the level but not the changes in the CAPM estimate of the cost of capital, and hence do not affect most of our conclusions.

7. We have made no attempt to incorporate the forecasts of investment advisory services in our DCF estimates. Although this could have been a useful approach to estimating the expected growth rate, we did not have the resources to gather and process the necessary data.

8. Some witnesses use the geometric rather than arithmetic mean to estimate the market risk premium. Others rely on actual market returns over a short sample period, such as five years. Both of these practices are mistakes and should not be followed.

9. See CRA 1984a for details. The most dramatic differences in the traditional and adjusted estimates of beta were in 1981, but all three rate-regulated industries had higher adjusted than traditional betas in every sample period, starting with 1962–1966 and ending with 1977–1981. The traditional and adjusted estimates for 1981 are: electric utilities, 0.32 (traditional) versus 0.68 (adjusted); gas distribution utilities, 0.89 versus 1.00; operating telephone companies (excluding AT&T), 0.30 versus 0.53; petroleum refining companies, 1.28 versus 1.12; pharmaceutical companies, 0.82 versus 0.91; and electronic computer companies, 0.88 versus 0.82.

10. The DCF growth rate also multiplies last year's dividend yield, and so any given change in the growth rate is slightly exaggerated in the final DCF estimate.

11. Current interest rates are not stable, so CAPM and other Risk Positioning estimates will vary with current capital market conditions, an advantage of these methods. The test proposed here is not stability of the final estimate but sensitivity to the precise choice of procedures used to estimate the key parameters.

12. The "midpoint" method refers to the choice of an average value from a range of reasonable estimates. It says nothing about how the range of estimates itself is determined.

Chapter 5

1. Robert Litzenberger has used the empirical CAPM several times.

2. Litzenberger, Ramaswamy, and Sosin (LRS) 1980 (p. 377) write and statistically estimate equation (5.2) with r_f subtracted from the left side instead of added to the right side. Our formulation is intended to facilitate comparison with (5.1).

3. The chief problem is that beta, a variable on the right side of the equation, is measured with error, so that an econometric problem known as "errors in the variables" arises. LRS apply one of the several methods that deal with this problem. For a summary of the various methods and a comparison of their results in a single rate-of-return application, see Pogue 1979b.

4. Note that a larger than average value for the bias naturally tends to lead to a high *book* rate of return, but this does not create a problem. The error in the book rate of return must not be correlated with the *true* rate of return.

5. Some harder-than-average statistical problems arise with this procedure; see Pogue 1979b for a more complete discussion. This equation looks like the ECAPM, for which the same statistical problems arise. It differs chiefly because Pogue uses EPR and DCF estimates of $E(r_j)$ instead of actual returns for company j over the period, and secondarily because Pogue did not subtract an estimate of r_f from his right-side variable before estimating a and b.

6. Pogue's procedure is also unusual in that he reports a *real* risk-return line and estimates the real rather than the nominal cost of capital.

7. Readers should be aware that one of the authors, and another member of the original CRA project team for the California PUC study, worked with Pogue during his analysis and provided assistance with some of the calculations and statistical analyses.

8. See Carleton 1982, who estimates beta using a number of explanatory variables, not just standard deviation of accounting rates of return.

9. Sharpe 1977.

10. Ross 1976a and 1976b.

11. However, the version of the APT equation presented here was developed by Ross and does use the market-risk premium.

12. Ross and Sharpe appear to have different attitudes about how a multifactor model should be constructed. Ross seems more concerned with untangling the information embodied in available data and less concerned with the economic interpretation of the underlying factors. Sharpe seems more interested in starting with a formal economic model and deriving the theoretically appropriate factors from it. It is not clear that this difference of opinion has much practical significance for rate testimony.

13. See Ross 1976a, p. 199, which uses somewhat different notation, and Sharpe 1977, equations (3), (14), and (25). Sharpe's paper does not report equation (5.5), but it is implied by the three equations referenced. See CRA 1982b, appendix B, for more discussion. Ross uses the expected return on a zero-beta portfolio in lieu of r_f, which is a generalization of little consequence for present purposes.

14. If there were more than one gamma but their relative sizes were fixed, there would be no way to distinguish between (5.1) and (5.5)—nor would there be any practical reason to do so.

15. Roll and Ross 1983 compare APT and CAPM estimates of the cost of equity for a number of utilities. They argue that the APT estimates, which are higher, should be preferred.

Appendix A

1. This statement and the remainder of this appendix assume that the firm is not in financial distress. The costs of financial distress tend to increase the cost of capital for highly leveraged firms. Since most managers recognize the dangers of excessive leverage, this condition is an anomaly. It usually occurs only when a severe business reversal results in a much higher degree of leverage. For discussion of the costs of financial distress, see Brealey and Myers 1981, chapter 18.

2. Since interest payments are fixed, the risk of fluctuations in the firm's overall revenues and operating income is borne by equityholders. Adding debt reduces the share of equity and thus increases the *relative* size of the *unchanged* variability of operating income compared to the *reduced* equity share of the assets.

3. As noted, if D/E is so high that the firm is in a position of financial distress, r will start to climb. This possibility is not reflected in figure A.1.

4. Strictly speaking, use of equation (A.1) (and the subsequent equations in this appendix) to adjust r_e for leverage assumes some fairly restrictive conditions, among them the *ex ante* equality of target and actual debt-equity ratios as measured by *market*, not book, values (see Myers 1974). Also, Miles and Ezzell 1980 recently showed that the basic formula is valid if the firm continually adjusts its *ex post* market-value debt-equity ratio to maintain the original target. See also Brealey and Myers (forthcoming), chapter 19. While the necessary assumptions are probably rarely met exactly in practice, we believe that these equations are sufficiently accurate for practical use in rate hearings, particularly since it often appears that no adjustment for differences in leverage is made at all. Therefore, the remainder of the appendix assumes that the necessary conditions are met, at least well enough for practical purposes.

5. This formula assumes that the tax shield provided by debt financing is perpetual and riskless. Neither assumption is correct; both tend to overstate the present value of tax shields.

6. Miller's conclusions have not gone unchallenged, however. See, for example, Modigliani 1982.

7. It can be shown that under the usual regulatory practice, the value of E in (A.3) will be smaller than in the unregulated case, in a way that makes r_e rise more rapidly than if equityholders were allowed to keep the expected value of the tax shields. In effect, ratepayers must compensate equityholders for the lost tax shields through a higher cost of equity than would otherwise be necessary. However, this creates no practical problems in using (A.3), be-

cause the value of E observed in the market (the market value of the regulated firm's stock) will be the correct value to use in (A.3). (Proof of this result is unpublished, but may be obtained from the authors on request.)

8. In contrast, if regulators were to reduce annual bills by a fixed amount (such as by cutting a customer's annual hook-up fee by his or her share of the interest tax shields), equityholders would never benefit from any part of the tax shields. Adding debt provides no advantage to equityholders, and equation (A.2) should be used instead of (A.3) for any regulated firm whose rates are set in this way, quite independently of whether the criticisms by Miller and others are correct. (Again, proof of this result is unpublished but may be obtained from the authors on request.)

9. For example, old issues of long-term debt, dating from times when interest rates were lower, sell at discounts from par or face value. Similarly, market and book values of stock may differ dramatically, especially for unregulated companies.

10. We stress again that t should be the *marginal* corporate tax rate. Also, r_d is not the embedded debt cost, but the average current yield to an investor buying Transylvania's debt at market value.

11. It is exactly offset if (A.2) is used instead of (A.3).

12. This table assumes that the cost of debt stays fixed as the debt ratio increases. This would happen if, for example, the debt were guaranteed by a parent firm. (Extremely high debt ratios supported by parent guarantees have been common in the oil pipeline industry due to a 1941 Consent Decree between major oil companies and the Department of Justice.) However, refer again to figure A.1. If a stand-alone company issued a very high proportion of debt, its debtholders would begin to bear risks usually borne by equityholders, so the cost of debt would go up rapidly and the cost of equity would not be as high as shown in this table.

13. We use the same tax rate, t, interest rate, r_d, and all-equity cost of capital, r, as in the previous numerical examples.

14. Once this is done, it can be seen that there is often little point to worrying about how much debt "should have" been used—the final cost to ratepayers is much the same.

Appendix B

1. As a practical matter, a commission would presumably set a return for all increments to book equity on a regular basis (e.g., annually), and then keep track of how much of that period's vintage remains in the rate base as depreciation accumulates.

2. Conventional utility stock is analogous to a variable rate bond, with periodic review of the expected rate of return to match current conditions, but still with uncertainty as to whether actual returns will meet expectations.

References and Additional Reading

Arzac, Enrique, R., and Matityahu Marcus. 1981. "Flotation Cost Allowance in Rate of Return Regulation: A Note." *Journal of Finance* 36:1199–1202. December.

Auerbach, Alan J. 1983. "Taxation, Corporate Financial Policy and the Cost of Capital." *Journal of Economic Literature* 21:905–940. September.

Averch, Harvey, and Leland Johnson. 1962. "Behavior of the Firm Under Regulatory Constraints." *American Economic Review* 52:1052–1069. December.

Bailey, Elizabeth E. 1973. *Economic Theory of Regulatory Constraint.* Lexington, Mass.: Lexington Books.

Bailey, Elizabeth E., and Roger D. Coleman. 1971. "The Effect of Lagged Regulation in an Averch-Johnson Model." *Bell Journal of Economics and Management Science* 2:278–292. Spring.

Banz, Rolf W. 1981. "The Relationship Between Return and Market Value of Common Stocks." *Journal of Financial Economics* 9:3–18. March.

Baumol, William J., and Alvin K. Klevorick. 1970. "Input Choices and Rate-of-Return Regulation: An Overview of the Discussion." *Bell Journal of Economics and Management Science* 1:162–190. Autumn.

Berry, William. 1983. "The Deregulated Electric Utility Industry." In *Electric Power Strategic Issues,* edited by James Plummer, Terry Ferrar, and William Hughes. Arlington, Va.: Public Utilities Reports, Inc. Palo Alto, Ca.: QED Research, Inc.

Bierman, Harold, Jr., and Jerome E. Hass. 1984. "Equity Flotation Cost Adjustments in Utilities' Cost of Service." *Public Utilities Fortnightly* 113:46–49. March.

Black, Fischer. 1972. "Capital Market Equilibrium with Restricted Borrowing." *Journal of Business* 45:444–455. July.

Black, Fischer, Michael C. Jensen, and Myron Scholes. 1972. "The Capital Asset Pricing Model: Some Empirical Tests." In *Studies in the Theory of Capital Markets,* edited by Michael C. Jensen. New York: Praeger.

Blume, Marshall. 1975. "Betas and Their Regression Tendencies." *Journal of Finance* 30:785–795. June.

Blume, Marshall. 1971. "On the Assessment of Risk." *Journal of Finance* 26:1–10. March.

Bodie, Zvi. 1976. "Common Stocks as a Hedge against Inflation." *Journal of Finance* 31:459–470. May.

Bower, Richard S. 1980. "Discussion." *Journal of Finance* 35:383–385. May.

Brealey, Richard, and Stewart C. Myers. 1984. *Principles of Corporate Finance.* 2d ed. New York: McGraw-Hill.

Brealey, Richard, and Stewart C. Myers. 1981a. *Principles of Corporate Finance.* New York: McGraw-Hill.

Brealey, Richard, and Stewart C. Myers. 1981b. *Instructor's Manual to Accompany Principles of Corporate Finance.* New York: McGraw-Hill.

Breen, William J., and Eugene M. Lerner. 1972. "On the Use of β in Regulatory Proceedings." *Bell Journal of Economics and Management Science* 3:612–621. Autumn.

Brennan, Michael J. 1981. "Discussion." *Journal of Finance* 36:352–353. May.

Brigham, Eugene F., and Roy L. Crum. 1977. "On the Use of CAPM in Public Utility Rate Cases." *Financial Management* 6:7–15. Summer.

Brown, Philip, Allan W. Kleidon, and Terry A. Marsh. 1983. "New Evidence on the Nature of Size-Related Anomalies in Stock Prices." *Journal of Financial Economics* 12:33–56.

Cagan, Phillip, and Robert E. Lipsey. 1978. *The Financial Effects of Inflation.* National Bureau of Economic Research General Series, no. 103. Cambridge, Mass.: Ballinger Publishing Co.

Carleton, Willard T., and Josef Lakonishock. 1982. *In the Matter of ITT World Communications Inc. Required Rate of Return.* ITT Worldcom Exhibit no. 3. Washington, D.C.: Federal Communications Commission.

Carleton, Willard T. 1974. "Rate of Return, Rate Base and Regulatory Lag Under Conditions of Changing Capital Costs." *Land Economics.* 145–151. May.

Charles River Associates (CRA). Forthcoming. *Choice of Discount Rates in Utility Planning: An Attempt to Estimate a Multi-Factor Model of the Cost of Equity Capital.* Palo Alto, Ca.: Electric Power Research Institute.

Charles River Associates. 1984a. *Choice of Discount Rates for Utility Planning: A Critique of Conventional Betas as Risk Indicators for Electric Utilities.* Palo Alto, Ca.: Electric Power Research Institute. February.

Charles River Associates. 1984b. *Generic Issues in Power Plant Phase-Ins.* Boston, Mass.: CRA. February.

Charles River Associates. 1982a. *Choice of Discount Rates in Utility Planning: Principles and Pitfalls*. Palo Alto, Ca.: Electric Power Research Institute. June.

Charles River Associates. 1982b. *Methods Used to Estimate the Cost of Equity Capital in Public Utility Rate Cases: A Guide to Theory and Practice*. Boston, Mass.: CRA. March.

Copeland, Thomas E., and J. Fred Weston. 1983. *Financial Theory and Corporate Policy*. 2d ed. Reading, Mass.: Addison-Wesley.

Farrar, Donald E., and Lee Selwyn. 1967. "Taxes, Corporate Financial Policy and Return to Investors." *National Tax Journal* 20:444–454. December.

Fama, Eugene F. 1981. "Stock Returns, Real Activity, Inflation and Money." *American Economic Review* 71:545–565. September.

Fama, Eugene F., and G. William Schwert. 1977. "Asset Returns and Inflation." *Journal of Financial Economics* 5:115–146. November.

Fama, Eugene F., and James D. Macbeth. 1973. "Risk, Return and Equilibrium: Empirical Tests." *Journal of Political Economy* 81:607–636. May-June.

Feldstein, Martin. 1980. "Inflation and the Stock Market." *The American Economic Review* 70:839–847. December.

Fisher, Franklin M., and John J. McGowan. 1983. "On the Misuse of Accounting Rates of Return to Infer Monopoly Profits." *The American Economic Review* 73:82–97. March.

Fisher, Franklin M., John J. McGowan, and Joen E. Greenwood. 1983. *Folded, Spindled, Mutilated: Economic Analysis and U.S. v. IBM*. Cambridge, Mass.: MIT Press.

Fogler, H. Russell, Kose John, and James Tipton. 1981. "Three Factors, Interest Rate Differentials and Stock Groups." *Journal of Finance* 36:323–335. May.

French, Walter G. 1981. "On the Attrition of Utility Earnings." *Public Utilities Fortnightly* 107:19–24. February.

Friend, Irwin. 1981. "Discussion." *Journal of Finance* 36:350–352. May.

Friend, Irwin, and Randolph Westerfield. 1980. "Co-Skewness and Capital Asset Pricing." *Journal of Finance* 35:897–913. September.

Golub, Bennet, and Leonard Hyman. 1983. "Financial Problems in the Transition to Deregulation." In *Electric Power Strategic Issues*, edited by James Plummer, Terry Ferrar, and William Hughes. Arlington, Va.: Public Utilities Reports, Inc. Palo Alto, Ca.: QED Research, Inc.

Golub, Bennet W., Richard D. Tabors, Roger E. Bohn, and Fred C. Schweppe. 1983. "An Approach for Deregulating the Generation of Electricity." In *Electric Power Strategic Issues*, edited by James Plummer, Terry Ferrar, and William Hughes. Arlington, Va.: Public Utilities Reports, Inc. Palo Alto, Ca.: QED Research, Inc.

Gordon, Myron J. 1977. "Comparison of Historical Cost and General Price

Level Adjusted Cost Rate Base Regulation." *Journal of Finance* 32:1501–1512. December.

Gordon, M. J. 1976. "The Current State of Rate of Return Regulation," paper read at FCC Conference on Future Planning, Washington, D.C., July.

Gottstein, Meg Schachter. 1983. "Discounted Cash Flow Cost of Capital Analysis." Staff Memo, Policy and Planning Division, California Public Utilities Commission. March 14.

Greenwald, Bruce C. 1980. "Admissable Rate Bases, Fair Rates of Return and the Structure of Regulation."*Journal of Finance* 35:359–368. May.

Hagerman, Robert L., and Brian T. Ratchford. 1978. "Some Determinants of Allowed Rates of Return on Equity to Electric Utilities." *The Bell Journal of Economics* 9:46–55. Spring.

Hendershott, Patric H. 1981. "The Decline in Aggregate Share Values: Taxation, Valuation Errors, Risk, and Profitability." *The American Economic Review* 71:909–922. December.

Higgins, Robert C. 1974. "Growth, Dividend Policy and Capital Costs in the Electric Utility Industry." *Journal of Finance* 29:1189–1201. September.

Holland, Daniel M., and Stewart C. Myers. 1980. "Profitability and Capital Costs for Manufacturing Corporations and All Nonfinancial Corporations." *The American Economic Review* 70:320–325. May.

Holland, Daniel M., and Stewart C. Myers. 1979. "Trends in Corporate Profitability and Capital Costs." in *The Nation's Capital Needs: Three Studies,* edited by Robert Lindsay. New York: Committee for Economic Development.

Hughes, William R. 1983. "Issues in Deregulation of Electric Generation." In *Essays in Honor of James Bonbright* edited by Albert Danielsen and David Kamerschen. Lexington, Mass.: Lexington Books.

Ibbotson, Roger G., and Rex A. Sinquefield. 1982. *Stocks, Bonds, Bills, and Inflation: The Past and The Future.* Charlottesville, Va.: Financial Analysts Research Foundation.

Ibbotson, Roger G., and Rex A. Sinquefield. 1979. "Stocks, Bonds, Bills and Inflation: Updates." *Financial Analysts Journal* 35:40–44. July-August.

Ibbotson, Roger G., and Rex A. Sinquefield. 1977. *Stocks, Bonds, Bills, and Inflation: The Past (1926–1976) and the Future (1977–2000).* Charlottesville, Va.: Financial Analysts Research Foundation.

Jensen, Michael, C., and William H. Meckling. 1976. "Theory of the Firm: Managerial Behavior, Agency Costs and Ownership Structure." *Journal of Financial Economics* 3:305–360. October.

Joskow, Paul L. 1974. "Inflation and Environmental Concern: Structural Change in the Process of Public Utility Price Regulation." *The Journal of Law and Economics* 17:291–327. October.

Joskow, Paul L. 1972. "The Determination of the Allowed Rate of Return in a Formal Regulatory Hearing." *The Bell Journal of Economics and Management Science* 3:632–644. Autumn.

Joskow, Paul L., and Richard Schmalensee. 1983. *Markets for Power: An Analysis of Electric Utility Deregulation.* Cambridge, Mass.: MIT Press.

Kahn, Alfred E. 1971. *The Economics of Regulation: Principles and Institutions.* 2 vols. New York: John Wiley & Sons.

Keynes, John Maynard. 1936. *The General Theory of Employment, Interest, and Money.* New York: Harcourt, Brace & World.

Kolbe, A. Lawrence. 1983. "Inflation-Driven Rate Shocks: The Problem and Possible Solutions." *Public Utilities Fortnightly* 111:26–34. February 17.

Kraus, Alan, and Robert H. Litzenberger. 1976. "Skewness Preference and the Valuation of Risk Assets." *Journal of Finance* 31:1085–1100. September.

Leland, Hayne E. 1974. "Regulation of Natural Monopolies and the Fair Rate of Return." *Bell Journal of Economics and Management Science* 5:3–15. Spring.

Lintner, John. 1965. "The Valuation of Risk Assets and the Selection of Risky Investments in Stock Portfolios and Capital Budgets." *Review of Economics and Statistics* 47:13–37. February.

Litzenberger, Robert, and Krishna Ramaswamy. 1979. "The Effect of Personal Taxes and Dividends on Capital Asset Prices: Theory and Empirical Evidence." *Journal of Financial Economics* 7:163–195. June.

Litzenberger, Robert, Krishna Ramaswamy, and Howard Sosin. 1980. "On the CAPM Approach to the Estimation of a Public Utility's Cost of Equity Capital." *Journal of Finance* 35:369–383. May.

Malkiel, Burton G. 1971. *The Debt Equity Combination of the Firm and the Cost of Capital: An Introductory Analysis.* New York: General Learning Press.

Markowitz, Harry M. 1952. "Portfolio Selection." *Journal of Finance* 7:77–91. March.

Marshall, William. 1980. "Discussion." *Journal of Finance* 35:385–387. May.

McDonald, John G. 1971. "Required Return on Public Utility Equities: A National and Regional Analysis, 1958–1969." *Bell Journal of Economics and Management Science* 2:503–514. Autumn.

Merton, Robert C. 1981. "On the Microeconomic Theory of Investment Under Uncertainty." In *Handbook of Mathematical Economics* edited by K. J. Arrow and M. D. Intriligator. Amsterdam: North-Holland Publishing Company.

Merton, Robert C. 1980. "On Estimating the Expected Return on the Market: An Exploratory Investigation." *Journal of Financial Economics* 8:323–361. December.

Miles, James A., and John R. Ezzell. 1980. "The Weighted Average Cost of

Capital, Perfect Capital Markets, and Project Life: A Clarification." *Journal of Financial and Quantitative Analysis* 15:719–730. September.

Miller, Merton H. 1977. "Debt and Taxes." *Journal of Finance* 32:261–275. May.

Miller, Merton H., and Franco Modigliani. 1967. "Some Estimates of the Cost of Capital to the Electric Utility Industry 1954–57: Reply." *American Economic Review* 57:1288–1300. December.

Miller, Merton H., and Franco Modigliani. 1966. "Some Estimates of the Cost of Capital to the Electric Utility Industry, 1954–57." *American Economic Review* 56:333–391. June.

Miller, Merton H, and Myron S. Scholes. 1982. "Dividends and Taxes: Some Empirical Evidence." *Journal of Political Economy* 90:1118–1141. December.

Modigliani, Franco. 1982. "Debt, Dividend Policy, Taxes, Inflation and Market Valuation." *Journal of Finance* 37:255–273. May.

Modigliani, Franco, and Richard A. Cohn. 1981. "A Reply." *Financial Analysts Journal* 37:72–73. May-June.

Modigliani, Franco, and Richard A. Cohn. 1979. "Inflation, Rational Valuation and the Market." *Financial Analysts Journal* 35:24–44. March-April.

Modigliani, Franco, and Merton H. Miller. 1969. "Reply to Heins and Sprenkle." *American Economic Review* 59:592–595. September.

Modigliani, Franco, and Merton H. Miller. 1963. "Corporate Income Taxes and the Cost of Capital: A Correction." *American Economic Review* 53:433–442. June.

Modigliani, Franco, and Merton H. Miller. 1958. "The Cost of Capital, Corporation Finance and the Theory of Investment." *American Economic Review* 48:261–297. June.

Mossin, Jan. 1966. "Equilibrium in a Capital Asset Market." *Econometrica* 34:768–783. October.

Myers, Stewart C. 1983. "The Search for Optimal Capital Structure." *Midland Corporate Finance Journal* 1:6–16. Spring.

Myers, Stewart C. 1979. *Verified Statement of Stewart C. Myers Before the U.S. Federal Energy Regulatory Commission.* Williams Pipeline Company, Docket no. OR79-1 *et al.* Filed July.

Myers, Stewart C. 1977. "Determinants of Corporate Borrowing." *Journal of Financial Economics* 5:147–175. November.

Myers, Stewart C. 1976. "Rate of Return Regulation—A Critical Appraisal." Paper read at FCC Conference on Future Planning. Washington, D.C. July 12.

Myers, Stewart C. 1974. "Interactions of Corporate Financing and Investment Decisions—Implications for Capital Budgeting." *Journal of Finance* 29:1–25. March.

Myers, Stewart C. 1973. "A Simple Model of Firm Behavior Under Regulation and Uncertainty." *Bell Journal of Economics and Management Science* 4:304–315. Spring.

Myers, Stewart C. 1972a. "On the Use of β in Regulatory Proceedings: A Comment." *Bell Journal of Economics and Management Science* 3:622–627. Autumn.

Myers, Stewart C. 1972b. "The Application of Finance Theory to Public Utility Rate Cases." *Bell Journal of Economics and Management Science* 3:58–97. Spring.

Myers, Stewart C., A. Lawrence Kolbe, and William B. Tye. Forthcoming. "Inflation and Rate of Return Regulation." *Research in Transportation Economics.*

Navarro, Peter, Bruce C. Peterson, and Thomas R. Stauffer. 1981. "A Critical Comparison of Utility-Type Ratemaking Methodologies in Oil Pipeline Regulation." *Bell Journal of Economics* 12:392–412. Autumn.

Oldfield, George S., Jr., and Richard J. Rogalski. 1981. "Treasury Bill Factors and Common Stock Returns." *Journal of Finance* 36:337–350. May.

Peseau, Dennis E., *et al.* 1978. "Utility Regulation and the CAPM: A Discussion." *Financial Management* 7:52–76. Autumn.

Pettway, Richard H. 1978. "On the Use of β in Regulatory Proceedings: An Empirical Examination." *Bell Journal of Economics* 9:239–248. Spring.

Pogue, Gerald A. 1979a. *Verified Statement of Gerald A. Pogue before the U.S. Federal Regulatory Commission.* Williams Pipeline Company, Docket no. OR79-1 *et al.* Filed July.

Pogue, Gerald A. 1979b. *Verified Supplemental Rebuttal Statement of Gerald A. Pogue before the U.S. Federal Energy Regulatory Commission.* Williams Pipeline Company, Docket no. OR79-1 *et al.* Filed October.

Plummer, James. 1983. "A Different Approach to Electricity Deregulation." In *Electric Power Strategic Issues,* edited by James Plummer, Terry Ferrar, and William Hughes. Arlington, Va.: Public Utilities Reports, Inc. Palo Alto, Ca.: QED Research, Inc.

Reinganum, Marc R. 1981a. "Misspecification of Capital Asset Pricing: Empirical Anomalies Based on Earnings, Yields and Market Values." *Journal of Financial Economics* 9:19–46. March.

Reinganum, Marc R. 1981b. "The Arbitrage Pricing Theory: Some Empirical Results." *Journal of Finance* 36:313–321. May.

Robichek, Alexander A. 1978. "Regulation and Modern Finance Theory." *Journal of Finance* 33:693–705. June.

Roll, Richard W. 1981. "A Possible Explanation of the Small Firm Effect." *Journal of Finance* 36:879–888. September.

Roll, Richard W. 1977. "A Critique of the Asset Pricing Theory's Tests." *Journal of Financial Economics* 4:129–176. March.

Roll, Richard W., and Stephen A. Ross. 1983. "Regulation, the Capital Asset and Pricing Model, and the Arbitrage Pricing Theory." *Public Utilities Fortnightly* 111:22–28. May.

Roll, Richard W., and Stephen A. Ross. 1980. "An Empirical Investigation of the Arbitrage Pricing Theory." *Journal of Finance* 35:1073–1103. December.

Ross, Stephen A. 1978. "The Current Status of the Capital Asset Pricing Model (CAPM)." *Journal of Finance* 33:885–901. June.

Ross, Stephen A. 1977. "Return, Risk and Arbitrage." In *Risk and Return in Finance*, vol. 1, edited by Irwin Friend and James L. Bicksler. Cambridge, Mass.: Ballinger Publishing Co.

Ross, Stephen A. 1976. "The Arbitrage Theory of Capital Asset Pricing." *Journal of Economic Theory* 13:341–360. December.

Sharpe, William F. 1964. "Capital Asset Prices: A Theory of Market Equilibrium Under Conditions of Risk." *Journal of Finance* 19:425–442. September.

Sharpe, William F. 1977. "The Capital Asset Pricing Model, a 'Multi-Beta' Interpretation." In *Financial Decision Making Under Uncertainty*, edited by Haim Levy and Marshall Sarnat. New York: Academic Press.

Solomon, Ezra. 1970. "Alternative Rate of Return Concepts and Their Implications for Utility Regulation." *Bell Journal of Economics and Management Science* 1:65–81. Spring.

Staff Study Group, U.S. Federal Energy Regulatory Commission. 1980. *Establishing the Rate of Return on Equity for Wholesale Electric Sales: Potential Regulatory Reforms*. Mimeographed. December 5.

Thompson, Howard E. 1979. "Estimating the Cost of Equity Capital for Electric Utilities: 1958-1976." *Bell Journal of Economics* 10:619–635. Autumn.

Thompson, Howard E., and Lionel W. Thatcher. 1973. "Required Rate of Return for Equity Capital Under Conditions of Growth and Consideration of Regulatory Lag." *Land Economics* 49:148–162. May.

Van Horne, James C. 1983. *Financial Management and Policy*. 6th ed. Englewood Cliffs, N.J.: Prentice-Hall, Inc.

Vasicek, Oldrich A. 1973. "A Note on Using Cross-Sectional Information in Bayesian Estimation of Security Betas." *Journal of Finance* 28:1233–1239. December.

Weidenbaum, Murray L. 1974. *Financing the Electric Utility Industry*. New York: Edison Electric Institute.

Weston, J. Fred, and Eugene F. Brigham. 1981. *Managerial Finance*. 7th ed. Hinsdale, Ill.: The Dryden Press.

Index